Thomas Jefferson
for Kids

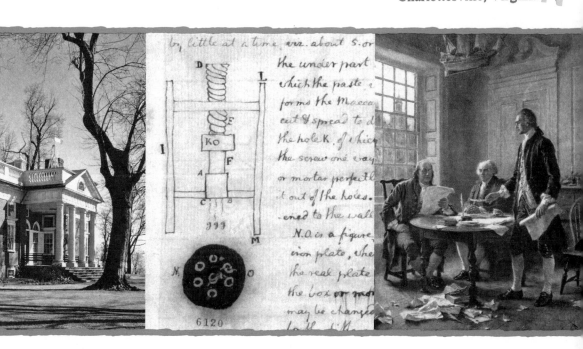

His Life and Times
with 21 Activities

CHICAGO
REVIEW
PRESS

BRANDON MARIE MILLER

LIBRARY OF CONGRESS CATALOGING-IN-PUBLICATION DATA
Miller, Brandon Marie.
    Thomas Jefferson for kids : his life and times, with 21 activities /
Brandon Marie Miller.
      p. cm.
    Includes bibliographical references and index.
    ISBN 978-1-56976-348-3
    1. Jefferson, Thomas, 1743–1826—Juvenile literature. 2. Jefferson,
Thomas, 1743–1826—Study and teaching (Elementary)—Activity
programs. 3. Presidents—United States—Juvenile literature.
4. Presidents—United States—Study and teaching (Elementary)—
Activity programs. I. Title.
    E332.79.M54 2011
    973.4'6092—dc23
    [B]
2011019318

© 2011 by Brandon Marie Miller
All rights reserved
Published by Chicago Review Press, Incorporated
814 North Franklin Street
Chicago, Illinois 60610
ISBN 978-1-56976-348-3
Printed in the United States of America
5 4 3 2 1

COVER AND INTERIOR DESIGN: Joan Sommers Design
INTERIOR ILLUSTRATIONS: TJ Romero
COVER IMAGES: (front top) Thomas Jefferson, original rough
draft of the Declaration of Independence, 1776, courtesy
of Library of Congress; (front center, left to right) Thomas
Jefferson, plan of the Federal District, 1791, courtesy of Library
of Congress; portrait of Thomas Jefferson from US two-dollar
bill, 1869, courtesy of Bureau of Engraving and Printing, US
Department of the Treasury; John Collier, Monticello, 1943,
courtesy of Library of Congress; Thomas Jefferson, drawing of pasta-making machine, 1787, courtesy of Library of
Congress; Jean Leon Gerome Ferris, *Writing the Declaration of
Independence, 1776*, c. 1932, courtesy of Library of Congress;
(back right) Cornelius Tiebout, *Thomas Jefferson: President of
the United States*, c. 1801, courtesy of Library of Congress

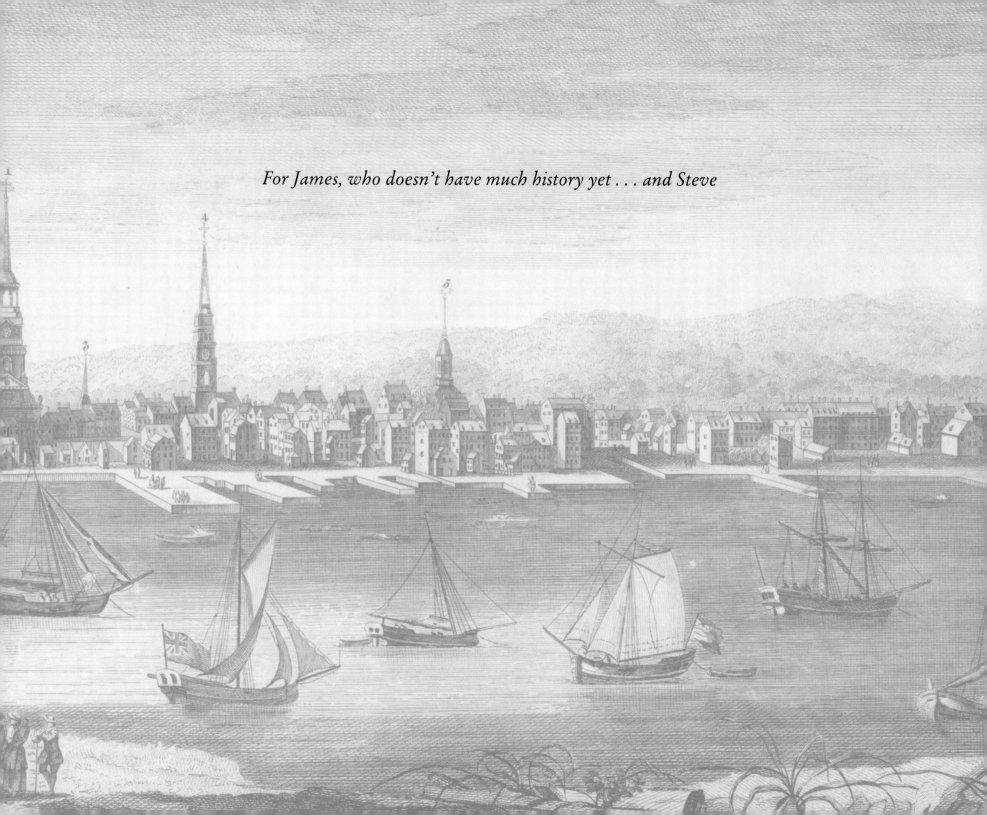

For James, who doesn't have much history yet . . . and Steve

CONTENTS

ACKNOWLEDGMENTS

Thank you to the Chael family for testing activities. Thank you to friends who listened to Jefferson stories: Neal and Justine Hendy, Cathy and John Berrens. Thank you to fellow writers Diana Jenkins and Kerrie Hollihan for hand-holding and encouragement. Thank you to the wonderful people who helped with illustrations. They keep American history alive and well with love and care. To Leah Stearns at the Thomas Jefferson Foundation, to Octavia Starbuck at Thomas Jefferson's Poplar Forest, to Marianne Martin at the Colonial Williamsburg Foundation, to Andrea Ashby at Independence National Historical Park, to Meghan Budinger at the James Monroe Museum. Also, thanks to Leandra Harrison DeFeo for sharing her intern experiences at Poplar Forest. Last, but never least, thank you to Paul.

TIME LINE

1743   April 13, born at Shadwell Plantation in Virginia

1757   Father Peter Jefferson dies

1760   Attends the College of William & Mary

1762   Studies law with George Wythe

1767   Begins law practice

1769   Building of Monticello under way; becomes member of House of Burgesses

1772   Marries Martha Wayles Skelton; daughter Martha (Patsy) born

1774   Writes a *Summary View of the Rights of British America*

1775   Serves in the Second Continental Congress

1776 Writes the Declaration of Independence and drafts for a new Virginia constitution

1777 Serves in Virginia House of Delegates; revises Virginia's state laws, proposes Virginia Statute for Religious Freedom

1778 Daughter Mary (Polly) born

1779–81 Governor of Virginia; begins writing *Notes on the State of Virginia*; flees from British invasion forces

1782 Wife Martha Jefferson dies after the birth of her sixth child

1784–89 Minister to France

1790–93 Serves as first US secretary of state; battles between Jefferson and Alexander Hamilton lead to the formation of political parties

1797–1801 Serves as vice president of the United States

1801–09 Serves as president of the United States

1803 United States purchases Louisiana Territory from France

1804 Daughter Mary dies

1804–06 Lewis and Clark expedition, launched by Jefferson to explore the Missouri River and beyond to the Pacific

1812 Renews friendship with John Adams after their political break a decade before

1815 Sells his library of nearly 6,700 volumes to Congress

1817–25 Plans and founds the University of Virginia

1826 Dies July 4 at Monticello, on the 50th anniversary of the Declaration of Independence

NOTE TO READERS

Thousands of Thomas Jefferson's letters and papers have survived for over 200 years. Throughout this book, many of the words you'll read were written by Jefferson himself, written in joy, in anger, in despair. Can you see Jefferson in flickering candle flame, dipping his quill pen in ink and writing the very words you read? Do you feel a connection to a real person? Think about it.

Research materials that actually come from a certain historic period, such as diaries, letters, paintings, clothes, tools, and newspapers, are called "primary sources." They were written or used by people of that time. Spelling, grammar, and punctuation have all changed over the centuries. Keep an eye out for these changes as you read.

"Bold in the Pursuit of Knowledge"

Peter Jefferson's wood-frame farmhouse overlooked the Rivanna River and vast tracts of green forest. In the distance rose the soft gray-blue silhouettes of Virginia's Blue Ridge Mountains. The house—called Shadwell—nestled in the Virginia wilderness. Hardy folk like Peter pushed west to settle the farthest reaches of British America, the perfect place for a self-made man. Peter Jefferson carved a farm from the forest, explored Virginia's frontier, and made a name for himself as a land surveyor and skilled mapmaker.

But Peter Jefferson had not chosen a "backcountry" woman for his wife. Instead, he'd courted a cousin of his good friend William Randolph. The sprawling Randolph clan boasted some of the best-educated, wealthiest, and most influential men in the colony. In 1739 Peter married 19-year-old

1

The house at Tuckahoe Plantation.

Jane Randolph. Jane's father, a planter and merchant, often dealt in human cargoes. His business sold Africans into slavery and poor Europeans as indentured servants.

The marriage connected the Jeffersons to one of Virginia's first families. Over the next 18 years Jane and Peter welcomed eight children to their clan, six daughters and two sons. Jane gave birth to her eldest son on April 13, 1743. They named the baby Thomas.

LIFE AT TUCKAHOE

When Thomas turned two, Peter's friend William Randolph died, leaving his three young children and his plantation, called Tuckahoe, in Peter's care. The Jefferson family left an overseer to run Shadwell and moved east. Thomas's first memory was the 50-mile ride to Tuckahoe, cradled on a pillow in front of one of Peter's slaves. Far grander than Shadwell, Tuckahoe stood a full two stories, an H-shaped white house with large rooms paneled in wood. For the next six years the Jeffersons called Tuckahoe their home.

Roughly 100 enslaved workers tilled Tuckahoe's fields and served the Jeffersons as cooks, maids, and craftsmen. Virginia planters depended on slave labor to plant, hoe, and harvest tobacco, the colony's main crop. Each year planters shipped barrels packed with crumbly dried tobacco leaves, good as cash, to agents in London. Planters instructed their agents to sell the tobacco, then buy and dispatch crates of goods back to the colony, crates of clothing, dishes, toys, tools, even carriages and harpsichords. The Jefferson family, like other Virginia planters, enjoyed comfortable lives on the labor of slaves. Thomas grew up in a world of master and slave, where an African American belonged to Peter Jefferson the same as a horse, a chair, or an acre of land.

As a boy Peter taught himself to read and write and vowed his own children would never lack for education. Peter hired a tutor, and young Thomas squeezed with the others into the cramped schoolroom near the main house, reciting drills in math, reading, and writing. Under their tutor's scrutiny they memorized lessons in religion and mastered penmanship with quill and ink. Thomas's quick mind delighted in words and numbers,

The Jefferson family enjoyed playing a board game called "The Royal Game of the Goose." This game had been around since the 1500s.

WHAT YOU NEED

2 or more people

Large sheet of poster board

Pencil

Colored markers

2 dice

Game pieces for each person (buttons, checkers, hard candies)

The game board is a spiral with 63 numbered sections. Following the diagram, draw the game board in pencil, then trace and color with markers. Mark a small number in each section. Some of the sections have hazards or benefits. Decorate the board as you wish. Include these:

- Space 6: "Bridge, advance to 12"

- Space 19: "The Inn, lose 1 turn"

- Space 31: "The Well, lose 2 turns"

- Space 42: "The Maze, go back to 30"

- Space 52: "The Prison, stay until next player lands, then go back to his/her space"

- Space 58: "Death, start over"

- Draw a goose on spaces: 5, 9, 14, 23, 36, 41, 54

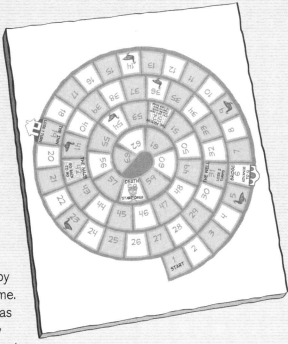

The object of the game is to travel along the spiral from 1 to 63. The first person to reach space 63 is the winner.

Going in turn, each player rolls the two dice and advances the sum of the two numbers. On the first roll there are two special combinations that let you jump ahead: if you roll 6 and 3 move to 26; if you roll 4 and 5 move to 53.

Two game pieces cannot occupy the same space at the same time. If you land on the same space as someone else, you get the new space and he or she must go back to the space where you started your turn.

If you land on a space with a goose, you get to move again by the same number as before. If you land on another goose, keep going.

To win you must land on space 63 with an exact count of the dice, but you can count only one die. If your number takes you over 63, then you must use the total of both dice, move forward and land on 63, and then go backward by the rest of your number. If you land on a goose, go back that same number again.

The one-room schoolhouse at Tuckahoe.

encouraged further as he noticed how his beloved father always had a book open or sat at his desk poring over his accounts, scratching sums with his quill pen. Jefferson family legend boasts that five-year-old Thomas soon read Peter's entire collection of books. True or not, Thomas's early passion for books never cooled.

With his siblings and Randolph cousins, Thomas rambled among the woods, fields, and rivers surrounding Tuckahoe, discovering the riches of nature. He learned to fish, swim, and ride a horse with grace and ease. Peter taught his son how to carefully measure and survey land, a practical skill

for any man, but especially for a lad who'd one day possess his own lands.

As much as Thomas basked in his father's company, Peter's growing wealth and reputation often pulled him away from home. Peter invested in a large land speculation company and spent much of his time exploring and surveying. In 1746–47 he mapped Virginia's "Northern Neck" for royal officials in Great Britain. As a man of means and position, Peter's neighbors elected him their representative in Virginia's legislature, the House of Burgesses, in the capital city of Williamsburg.

HOME TO SHADWELL

When the oldest Randolph son, Thomas Mann, turned 12, Peter moved his family back home to Shadwell to better tend nine-year-old Thomas's education. In 1752 Peter enrolled his son in a boarding school run by the Reverend William Douglas. For the next five years, Thomas acquired a basic gentleman's education, reading Greek and Latin, and a smattering of French.

Most spare hours Thomas spent playing his violin. Self-taught, he both played by ear and read music. If he heard a piece played on the harpsichord, he could transpose the notes for violin. On visits home, he loved accompanying his favorite sibling, Jane, while she sang.

With his large family overflowing Shadwell, Peter began expanding his home in 1753. Thomas's weekend visits found his family deep in the midst of stacks of bricks and dust and mortar, grating saws, and ringing hammers. But he had little time with

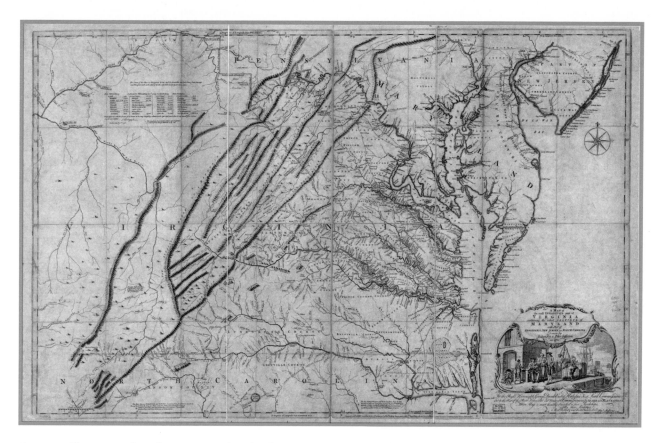

Peter Jefferson and Joshua Fry make the first accurate map of Virginia, 1751.

COURTESY OF LIBRARY OF CONGRESS

his father. The land speculation business kept Peter absent nearly four days a week. A man on the move, he also served his fellow westerners as a justice of the peace, sheriff, and militia officer.

Then on August 17, 1757, Peter Jefferson suddenly died at age 49. His father's death staggered 14-year-old Thomas, who felt "the whole care and direction of myself was thrown on myself entirely." He buried himself in a refuge of books and music, seeking comfort.

THE YOUNG SCHOLAR

Peter had named friends to oversee his finances and serve as guardians to his children. To Thomas, his eldest son, Peter left Shadwell, half of his 7,500 acres, the choice of two plantations, his best body servant, and 25 more slaves—all this would become Thomas's on his 21st birthday. Thomas also inherited his father's library of 40 books, his bookcase, cherry writing desk, and surveying tools. Thomas's brother Randolph also received land and

Jefferson was a trained surveyor, so maps played an important role in his life. His father, Peter, was "employed . . . to make the 1st map of Virginia which had ever been made." Later, as president, Jefferson doubled the size of the country with the Louisiana Purchase (1803) and sent Lewis and Clark to start mapping the west (1804–06).

WHAT YOU NEED

Tape measure

Your backyard or a section of a park

Ruler

Sheet of watercolor paper

Pencils

Markers

Watercolor paints and brush

Decide what scale you will use to create your map. Use the tape measure to measure across your backyard. How many feet is it? Now, according to your ruler, how many inches across is your paper? Divide the number of feet by the number of inches. For example, the yard measures 120 feet across and the paper is 14 inches across: 120 divided by 14 = 8½. To make things easier, pick a nice even number slightly less than you calculated. On this example map, every inch will equal 8 feet. That is the scale. In the corner of your map, write down what the scale is. Now you can measure out your yard to scale size using the tape measure.

Put in major items that shape the yard, such as the driveway, flower beds, patio, or deck. Label these in small print.

Note where smaller items appear in the yard: bird-bath, swing set, rocks, bushes, picnic table, etc.

Where do they fit into the scale measure of the yard? Design an icon for things that appear several times in the yard: trees, bushes, flowers, ornamental grasses, and make a key. Draw the icons on your map.

Use a wet brush dipped in watercolors to lightly tint your map. Be sure to include an arrow pointing north so that a map reader can hold the map and know if he or she is facing the right direction.

For additional fun, use the map for a scavenger hunt. Hide a variety of small items around the yard—for instance, a Jefferson nickel, a feather, something red, a blue balloon, a stick, two different leaves, an acorn, a pinecone, something soft, a button, a pencil, a piece of yarn or string, a photo of Monticello (printed from online), a $2 bill with Jefferson's image, a plastic spoon, etc. Divide your friends into two teams, and give each team a copy of your map, a bag, and a list of the hidden items. Use a watch to time your friends as they search for the items and put them in the bag. They must mark on their copy of the map where they find each item. Give them 5 to 10 minutes to complete the hunt.

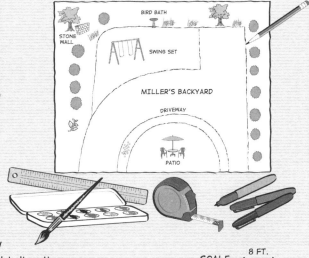

SCALE   8 FT.

DIRECTION   N

LABEL

     MILLER'S BACKYARD

KEY

   BUSHES, PLANTS

   TREE

   STONES

   IVY

a plantation. The Jefferson daughters received no property but would get dowries when they married. Jane was only 37 when Peter died and left her with eight children. Peter granted his wife the use of one-third of his property and Shadwell's house and farm until her death or remarriage.

After Peter's death Thomas entered a new school about 12 miles from Shadwell run by the Reverend James Maury. The Jeffersons paid Reverend Maury £22 worth of tobacco a year for Thomas's education. As the eldest son, Thomas returned home on the weekends to help his mother, sometimes bringing a friend like Dabney Carr. With Thomas's sisters, Martha and Jane, they hiked and rode horseback, played music, and sang. One story tells of Carr challenging Thomas to a horse race. Carr owned a sleek racehorse guaranteed to beat Thomas's fat old mare. Thomas set the race date for February 30—a day that did not exist, and avoided the race completely!

Reverend Maury encouraged Thomas's natural talent for languages. Over the next two years his hungry pupil devoured the classics, books by Homer, Plato, Livy, and Cicero, read in Latin. Maury pushed Thomas to hone his writing skills and "natural philosophy"—science. Best of all for bookworm Thomas, Maury possessed a library of 400 titles. Thomas not only threw himself into his studies but often practiced his violin up to three hours a day as well.

Teenage Thomas grew into a tall, gangly, string bean of a youth. He eventually stood six feet two inches tall. Thomas's red hair, as well as his height, singled him out. Shy and soft-spoken, he sometimes mumbled and hated to speak in public. Not close to his mother, after Peter's death he remained often away from Shadwell, immersing himself in school.

Death ran like a dark river through the commonplace book where Thomas, frequently secretive and gloomy after Peter's passing, copied passages from literature that touched him. From Horace's *Odes* he wrote, "Pale Death with foot impartial knocks at the poor man's cottage and at princes' palaces." In another passage about fleeting time and looming separation, a melancholy Jefferson copied lines from Laurence Sterne's *Tristram Shandy*: "Time wastes too fast! . . . The days and hours of it . . . are flying over our heads like light clouds of a windy day never to return more!"

"BY GOING TO THE COLLEGE"

By January 1760 17-year-old Thomas longed for a change. He wrote his guardian John Harvie seeking permission to leave Reverend Maury and attend the College of William & Mary in Williamsburg.

> ## The Classics
>
> When people talked about the classics, they meant writings from ancient Rome and Greece—the histories, philosophy, and literature that had given birth to Western civilization. To read something "in the original" meant you read it in Greek or Latin, or even ancient Hebrew. Phrases in Latin and Greek dot Thomas's early letters as he claimed his place as a young gentleman of knowledge.

"By going to the College," Thomas presented his case, "I shall get a more universal Acquaintance which may hereafter be serviceable to me. . . . I can pursue my Studies in the Greek & Latin as well there as here, & likewise learn something of the Mathematics."

His guardians agreed to the plan, and in spring 1760 Thomas set out on horseback, his slave Jupiter riding alongside, for the 150-mile trip to Williamsburg. On the way he met Patrick Henry, seven years older than Thomas and heading to the capital to study law. They discovered a shared love of the violin. Their paths would cross many times over the years.

Thomas rode into Williamsburg and discovered the grandest town he'd ever seen, a hive of 200 houses and 2,000 residents. Enslaved workers made up half the town's population. Thomas arrived during the legislative season, when the capital hummed with business and pleasure. The mile-long stretch of Duke of Gloucester Street between the Capitol Building, where the House of Burgesses met, and the College of William & Mary, bustled with people and carriages. Taverns and shops lured visitors with the promise of rich fare and gossip or the latest goods, fresh from England. Wealthy planters who kept a home in Williamsburg to enjoy the social season hoped to show off their silk and velvet finery, their best wigs, and their most graceful dance steps at the Governor's Palace. Virginians loved dances, horse races, and gambling, betting large sums on cards, dice, and cockfights.

COLLEGE LIFE

Many of the college's 100 male students arrived more prepared to party and woo young ladies than study. Thomas joined the amusements, too, slipping into dances at the Raleigh Tavern's Apollo Room, and he especially loved horses and horseracing. He attended plays performed by traveling companies from London and New York. Though Thomas carefully tallied his expenses in a ledger, money vanished from his pocket, spent on clothes, a new horse, and entertainment with close friends Dabney Carr and John Page. Thomas's blood ties to the Randolphs earned him invitations to the beautiful homes of Virginia's influential families.

But these diversions didn't distract Thomas from studying, sometimes 15 hours a day, poring over his books in flickering candlelight while his fellow students snored in their beds. Thomas balanced his rigorous studies with exercise whenever possible, hiking, swimming, riding horseback, and even soaking his feet in cold water each morning as a health booster.

The college did not require students to attend lectures—the young men showed up or not. Church attendance every Sunday was required, however, and Thomas shuffled into the pews at Bruton Parish Church alongside the rest of the students. Part of William & Mary's mission was training future Church of England, or Anglican, ministers. Thomas's mind, so eager to grasp new knowledge, swayed toward the school of philosophy, not the divinity school.

School breaks meant a return to Shadwell. Thomas often hiked the surrounding hills. He dreamed of building his own home someday on this land his father had left him, overlooking mountains and valleys. Shadwell, after all, would house his mother and younger siblings for many years. Thomas spent hours shut away studying, plagued

The Age of Enlightenment

Jefferson, like other scholars of the 18th century, believed in the use of reason. Human beings could understand the natural world through science, through observation and evidence. They also believed that natural laws governed people, just as natural laws governed the universe. Jefferson had faith that humans, as reasonable creatures, could ride a wave of science and learning to a new plateau of progress. People would choose happiness and goodness if left free to soar above the chains of kings, powerful government, and church rulers.

by boredom with life at home. Everything "trudged on in one and the same round," he complained to John Page. "We rise in the morning that we may eat breakfast, dinner and supper, and we go to bed again that we may get up the next morning and go the same, so that you never saw two peas more alike than our yesterday and today." He felt much happier back at school.

The College of William & Mary, from The Bodleian Plate, *around 1740.*
THE COLONIAL WILLIAMSBURG FOUNDATION

★ ACTIVITY ★ DANCE A REEL

Dancing served as a main form of entertainment and socializing in Virginian society. Dances, also called assemblies, were places to see others and be seen. Mastery of intricate dance steps required lessons with dancing masters or studying diagrammed books with dance steps and rules. Jefferson attended many dances while a student in Williamsburg. Country-dances, such as reels, were fast-paced, with as many couples "as will" joining in, facing each other in rows.

WHAT YOU NEED

At least 4 couples

Music (look online for music samples; try a lively hornpipe or the tune for Sir Roger de Coverley)

Couples form two lines facing each other. (Wearing long dresses and knee breeches is optional!) Steps are done quickly and lightly on the toes or balls of the feet. *Do-si-do* ("dough-see-DOUGH") is when a couple pass each other, shoulder to shoulder, and without turning, continue around each other back-to-back. *Chassé* ("sha-SAY") is when you gallop sideways, one foot "chasing" the other.

There is a Head Couple, the pair at the very front of each line, and a Foot Couple, the pair at the very back. In this activity, you will use the terms *gentleman* and *lady*. The Head Lady and Foot Gentleman move diagonally and meet in the middle, bow and curtsy, and move back to the starting place. This is called *forward and back*. Next, the Head Gentleman and Foot Lady do the same.

DO-SI-DO

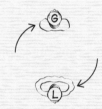

G = GENTLEMAN
L = LADY

FIRST MOVE

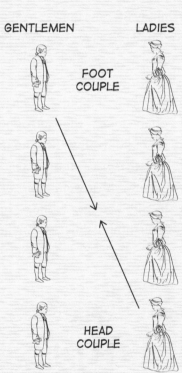

GENTLEMEN

LADIES

FOOT COUPLE

HEAD COUPLE

The Head Lady and Foot Gentleman come forward, join right hands at shoulder level, make one complete turn, and return to their places. The Head Gentleman and Foot Lady then do the same.

The Head Lady and Foot Gentleman come forward again, join hands, and make a complete turn, then go back to their places. The Head Gentleman and Foot Lady do the same.

The Head Lady and Foot Gentleman come forward, do-si-do starting right shoulder to right shoulder, and go back. The Head Gentleman and Foot Lady do the same. Both couples repeat a do-si-do in the opposite direction, starting left shoulder to left shoulder.

The Head Couple join hands and chassé down the center of the lines, then return to the starting place. The Head Couple then link arms and circle one and a half times around. The Head Lady faces the gentlemen's line and the Head Gentleman faces the ladies' line. The Head Lady links arms with the second gentleman and turns him once; the Head Gentleman does the same with the second lady.

The Head Couple return to the middle, link right arms, and turn each other once, then turn the third gentleman and third lady and continue down until they reach the foot of the line.

At the foot of the line the Head Couple join raised hands to form an arch. The other couples join hands, march through the arch, split off, and go up the sides. The Head Couple now become the Foot Couple, and the second couple are now the new Head Couple. Repeat the dance until all the couples have moved through the line.

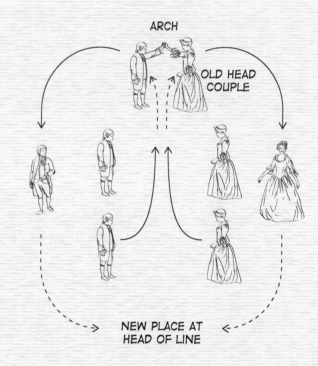

LAST MOVE

ARCH

OLD HEAD COUPLE

NEW PLACE AT HEAD OF LINE

The Governor's Palace in Williamsburg, symbol of British authority.

In Williamsburg the promising, hardworking student drew the notice of Professor William Small, a young Scotsman who taught mathematics and physics. Thomas admired Small's gentlemanly manners and "enlarged and liberal mind" that opened doors of new thought to Thomas. Dr. Small tutored him in science and encouraged his love for math. Thomas later recalled, "When I was young, mathematics was the passion of my life." Small also owned a collection of fascinating scientific instruments and introduced his brightest pupil to the writings of enlightened thinkers such as Voltaire, Rousseau, and Montesquieu.

Small also dragged along his freckled, lanky student on visits to Governor Francis Fauquier, where music, politics, and science dominated dinner discussions. Jefferson even played concerts at the Governor's Palace, joined by musicians on the cello, flute, and harpsichord. He later recalled, "It was my great good fortune," one that "probably fixed the destinies of my life" when he met Dr. Small. And it was through William Small that Jefferson met his life's greatest mentor, the legal scholar George Wythe.

READING LAW

A leading lawyer in the colony and in his late 30s, Wythe owned a large brick home facing Palace Green, just a moment's stroll from the gates of the Governor's Palace. After two years at William & Mary, Thomas left the college to study law with Mr. Wythe.

At the time, no law schools existed. Instead a student "read law" with a member of the bar, working through stacks of books, legal treatises, and contracts. Eventually graduating to the level of an unpaid clerk, students copied out piles of writs—the legal documents used in lawsuits—hoping that each stroke of the pen etched the forms and language of law into the brain. When the would-be young lawyer felt ready, usually after about two years, he appeared for questioning before the bar. If he passed, the student became a full-fledged lawyer. Patrick Henry read law for only six weeks. Thomas, the young man who loved learning above all else, studied with George Wythe for *five years*! Jefferson remembered

Born in Virginia in 1726, George Wythe [pronounced "with"] became a leading scholar, lawyer, legislator, and judge. His law students included not only Jefferson but also future chief justice of the United States John Marshall. A supporter of American liberties, Wythe helped steer Virginia's course toward revolution. As a delegate to the Second Continental Congress, he signed the Declaration of Independence, the greatest work of his former student Thomas Jefferson.

Wythe helped write the new Virginia state constitution and served on the committee that revised Virginia's code of laws. In 1777 he became the new nation's first professor of law at the College of William & Mary, and later served as a judge.

A childless widower, Wythe willed his legal books to Jefferson and his property to a grandnephew, George Wythe Sweeney, and also provided money to his freed slaves Mathew Brown and Lydia Broadnax. Sweeney, greedy for cash, forged checks with Wythe's name and then resorted to murder to cover his tracks. In 1806 Sweeney poisoned the food of his uncle and Mathew Brown, killing them both. Sweeney was charged with murder, but eventually set free because no witness saw him poison the food. Lydia Broadnax may have known what happened, but as an African American she could not testify in court against a white person.

Wythe was, wrote Jefferson, "my faithful and beloved Mentor in youth, and my most affectionate friend through life." On another occasion, he wrote, "No man left behind him a character more venerated. His virtue was of the purest tint . . . his unaffected modesty . . . endeared him to every one. . . . Such was George Wythe, the honor of his own, and model of future times."

George Wythe, Jefferson mentor and friend.
COURTESY OF THE COLONIAL WILLIAMSBURG FOUNDATION, GIFT OF THE VESTRY OF BRUTON PARISH CHURCH

Jefferson danced at the Apollo Room in the Raleigh Tavern and later attended unauthorized meetings here after the royal governor shut down the House of Burgesses.

THE COLONIAL WILLIAMSBURG FOUNDATION

those years fondly, "a time of life," he wrote, "when I was bold in the pursuit of knowledge."

Under Wythe's supervision Jefferson read history, philosophy, and ethics as well as law. Jefferson analyzed and pondered volumes of English law recounting centuries of court cases and legal opinions. He studied parliamentary law, learning how to conduct the business and debates of a legislature. Jefferson read civil law cases involving issues such

as land ownership and inheritance. Jefferson needed nearly a year to plow through Sir Edward Coke's gigantic volumes on the whole of English law. "I do wish the Devil had old Coke," Jefferson wrote John Page, "for I am sure I never was so tired of an old dull scoundrel in my life."

Jefferson's day began at five o'clock in the morning when he read "ethics, religion, and natural law" until eight o'clock. From eight until noon he concentrated on his legal studies. After lunch he read political theories by writers like John Locke and Montesquieu. Late afternoon he paused for a meal or conversation, or read Greek and Roman history in the original language. In the evenings he practiced his writing, learning how to craft a clear argument, or sharpened his speaking skills, something the shy young man never quite mastered. Jefferson found time to teach himself Italian after attending an Italian opera, and his beloved violin rested never far from hand. He also indulged his new obsession: buying and collecting books.

TOO SHY FOR LOVE

In 1762, 19-year-old Thomas fell smitten with Rebecca Burwell, age 16. His great shyness prevented the first-year law student from even speaking to Rebecca for over a year. Instead, he talked and wrote about her to his friends.

When he finally worked up the courage to speak to her, Thomas asked Rebecca to cut a silhouette of herself for him to carry in the back of his watch. But his bedroom's leaky roof ruined the picture. Even without the silhouette, "there is so lively an image of her imprinted in my mind that I shall think of her too often, I fear, for my peace of mind." It would look bad asking her for another silhouette "after my suffering the other to get spoiled," he wrote John Page.

Thomas finally had his chance to dance with Rebecca in October 1763. The couple met at the Apollo Room in the Raleigh Tavern. But the evening dashed Thomas's hopes.

I was prepared to say a great deal. I had dressed up in my own mind such thoughts . . . in as moving language as I knew how, and expected to have performed in a tolerably creditable manner. But, Good God! When I had an opportunity of venting them, a few broken sentences, uttered in great disorder and interrupted with pauses of uncommon length were the too visible marks of my strange confusion!

Page encouraged Jefferson to court Rebecca. But Jefferson feared rejection, which would "be ten times more wretched," than if he said nothing. Rebecca offered him no encouragement; he soon heard she planned to marry someone else. Jefferson returned to his law studies and banished the idea of marriage for many years.

POLITICAL RUMBLINGS

When George Wythe attended sessions of the General Court (the highest court in Virginia) or county courts, or served as a member of the House of Burgesses, Thomas trailed along acting as clerk, taking notes, studying, copying out legal documents, and learning how to make a case on his own. Through this hands-on experience Jefferson learned the laws of Virginia and Great Britain.

All was not well, however, between Great Britain and her colonies. Needing to raise money after victory in the French and Indian War, the British Parliament passed a series of new tax laws. This time the crown determined the American colonies would pay their fair share. But colonists,

Patrick Henry speaks before the House of Burgesses on the Stamp Act.
COURTESY OF LIBRARY OF CONGRESS

who had no representatives voting in the British Parliament, had only paid taxes passed by their own colonial legislatures. A crisis erupted with the passage of the Stamp Act in 1765. The act would tax all papers and documents, even playing cards. Angry mobs attacked stamp tax collectors and destroyed property in cities up and down the Atlantic coast.

On May 29, 1765, Jefferson hovered in the doorway of the House of Burgesses and listened to the debate inside. In a blazing speech, Patrick Henry denied British authority to tax the colonists, claiming only the general assembly of the colony had that right. Parliament's actions, challenged Henry, would "destroy British as well as American freedom." King George III had better be careful, Henry warned. Cries of treason shouted Henry down, but Henry boldly answered, "If this be treason, make the most of it!" To Jefferson, Henry's passion-filled arguments showed powers "such as I have never heard from any other man."

FAMILY LIFE

Jefferson also spent time at Shadwell, tending to family matters and studying on his own. He'd come into his inheritance at age 21 in 1764 and now managed his own affairs. He began keeping detailed account books of what he spent and what he earned. Like most planters Jefferson rarely had cash on hand; his wealth existed mostly in land and property, including his slaves. Tobacco required much labor, and the greedy weed quickly sucked nutrients from the soil. Virginia's planter elite, including Jefferson, needed to add acres of fresh land to their holdings, often borrowing money to make purchases. Even at this young age Jefferson felt the burden of debt.

One happy event occurred in July 1765 when Thomas's close friend Dabney Carr married Thomas's 19-year-old sister Martha. Thomas's older sister Jane, however, had reached the age of 25 still unmarried, earning the unwanted and scornful titles of spinster or old maid. But Jane, bright, sweet, and a lovely singer, was Thomas's favorite. Sadly, only a few months after Martha's wedding, Jane Jefferson died on October 1. Her death crushed Thomas. He wrote in Latin across the pages of his account book:

Jane Jefferson

Ah, Jane, best of girls!
Flower snatched away in its bloom!
May the earth weigh lightly upon you!
Farewell for a long, long time.

Thomas had longed to travel. Jane's death pushed him to actually go. From May through August 1766 he traveled north to visit Annapolis, where he joined celebrations over the repeal of the Stamp Act, then on to Philadelphia and New York City. Thomas especially savored the architecture and gardens and thoroughly enjoyed sightseeing and shopping in cities that dwarfed Williamsburg in size. Then he headed home to Virginia—time to settle down as a practicing lawyer!

Clearing the Rivanna River

Like other planters, Jefferson knew that his crop did him no good if he couldn't get it to market. Many of Virginia's great plantations settled along rivers for fast, cheap, and easy access to Atlantic shipping. But in Jefferson's case, the Rivanna River only carried his goods so far before rocks barred the way. His goods had to be hauled overland to the James River, at great expense of time and money.

Jefferson explored the Rivanna in a canoe. He determined that if some boulders could be removed, the Rivanna could carry his goods all the way to the James, then onto ships to cross the sea to England. By 1765 Jefferson organized his neighbors, raised money from private subscribers, and received the go-ahead from the House of Burgesses. The river project took five years to complete. Even decades later, after so many successes, Jefferson remained proud of his first public project.

In 1767 he appeared with George Wythe before the bar. Wythe swore that his clerk was honorable, able, and well trained. A committee of examiners asked Jefferson a few legal questions, he took an oath of membership, and he dined with Wythe and the bar examiners. He could now try cases before the General Court. He'd spent his life from age 19 to 24 immersed in the law and learning. Now, with his brilliant legal mind and family connections to help his rise in Virginia society, Thomas Jefferson had at his fingertips everything he needed to succeed.

BUTCHER'S HALL

CUSTOM HOUSE

"His Majesty Has No Right"

As the next years unfolded, Thomas Jefferson pressed hard to earn a reputation as one of Virginia's elite young lawyers. He was the only General Court lawyer practicing in western Virginia. The job demanded hours in the saddle clomping over mountains and rough roads. Jefferson shuffled his time between Shadwell, Virginia's western counties for court sessions, and Williamsburg, where the General Court met twice a year.

Court days lured people from the countryside, entertainers strutted on makeshift stages, gamblers enticed with cockfights and cards, and most anything might be bought or sold: food and drink, cattle, hogs—and slaves. Criminal and civil cases turned jammed courtrooms into entertainment. Many traveled for miles to file land claims and pay fees.

A lot of Jefferson's cases involved frontier land patents. Anyone could survey land and file a fee. But if they did not use the land within a certain time their claim could be challenged, resulting in a mountain of legal cases over land disputes.

Jefferson also represented some of Virginia's most prominent citizens, like William Byrd III, the colony's largest landowner. His legal travels allowed Jefferson to visit old friends and forge new contacts. He most treasured quiet evenings talking literature, philosophy, and politics or playing chess and listening to music. The lavish lifestyles enjoyed in the fine homes of these gentlemen planters rubbed off. Jefferson became "an admirer of elegance and convenience," noted Jefferson's cousin Edmund Randolph.

Jefferson dressed well, often favoring a red waistcoat over his breeches and fine white stockings, his feet clad in shoes sporting silver buckles. In Williamsburg he dined at the Raleigh Tavern, sipped coffee at Mrs. Vobe's coffeehouse, and attended performances at the playhouse. Jefferson pursued other entertainments, too—he paid to view an elk, a tiger, puppet shows, and a magician, and bet on horse races. He played his violin and caught musical shows, including a performance on the glass armonica, an instrument invented by Benjamin Franklin. People noted how music often claimed Jefferson body and soul; he always hummed or sang softly striding down the street.

Though Jefferson handled over 930 cases during his law career, he viewed himself more as a gentleman planter than a working lawyer. He found probing questions of law and preparing legal arguments interested him far more than arguing cases in a courtroom. Still, the law practice sometimes earned half his income.

MONTICELLO

Jefferson undertook several momentous steps in 1769. He had decided to leave Shadwell and create his own home. He chose a piece of land, an 867-foot-tall hilltop a few miles away, left to him by his father. From here Jefferson looked out over rolling fields, forests, and mountains, with the Rivanna River running like a thin silver-green ribbon in the distance. Jefferson called his new home by the Italian word for "little mountain": Monticello.

Jefferson designed his new home himself, searching books on architecture and design patterns for inspiration. He especially loved the classical architecture of ancient Rome, newly interpreted during the 16th-century Italian Renaissance. He pored over the architectural books of Andrea Palladio, published in 1570, praising the volumes as his architectural bible. Jefferson's plan called for a library, a dining room, a parlor, bedrooms, and outbuildings for the kitchen, laundry, storehouses, and workshops.

In 1768 he'd had the mountaintop cleared and leveled. The next year brick-making began at the site. Jefferson figured that building Monticello would require about 310,000 bricks. "This winter is employed," he wrote a friend, "in getting framing [wood], limestone and [in] bringing up stone for the foundation."

He hired skilled white craftsmen, assisted by a few trained slaves and other enslaved laborers. The

Italian architect Andrea Palladio's (1508–80) interpretation of classical Greek and Roman architecture greatly influenced Thomas Jefferson. One of Palladio's trademark designs was an arched window.

ADULT SUPERVISION REQUIRED

WHAT YOU NEED

2 sheets of foam board

Tape measure, ruler, or yardstick

Pencil

Utility knife

Sheets of clear cellophane

Glue

Thick black marker

Scissors, if needed

Draw a window design on one sheet of foam board using a tape measure, a pencil, and the illustration below for guidance. Then use a utility knife to cut out the windowpane shapes.

On the back of the window, glue the sheets of cellophane (cut slightly bigger than the pane) onto the frames. In the space around the window, use a thick black marker to draw other Palladian elements, such as pilasters on the sides and the stones around the arch with the keystone in the center.

Cut wedges from the second foam-board sheet. Glue the wedges on the bottom of the window to act as feet for standing it up.

in architecture" he wrote, continued on and off for decades as he built, tore down, expanded, and refined his world.

In 1770 a fire destroyed Shadwell, along with most of Jefferson's personal and legal papers and his treasured books. His mother and sisters crowded into the outbuildings and eventually moved to live with Jane's brother. Jefferson estimated he'd lost about £200 worth of books. He suffered the loss greatly, writing John Page, "Would to God it had been the money; then had it never cost me a sigh!" He felt "destitute" that his prized collection had "perished in the flames." He began at once to piece together his legal notes and papers and rebuild his library, snatching up law books as well as volumes on philosophy, politics, history, and poetry, and novels.

By November 1770 Jefferson moved into one of the few finished spaces at Monticello, a little brick cottage on the South Pavilion. The one room "serves me for parlor, for kitchen and hall, I may add for bed chamber and study, too. . . . I have hope, however of getting more elbow room this summer."

THE HOUSE OF BURGESSES

As Monticello rose on the mountaintop, in May 1769 Jefferson strode onto the stage of politics. Elected to represent Albemarle County, he took his seat in the House of Burgesses. Jupiter again accompanied Jefferson to Williamsburg, where he was sworn in at the Capitol. At the opening session the king's representative, Governor Botetourt, arrived grandly in a coach pulled by six white horses. As the oldest representative government in the colonies,

A reconstruction of the colonial Capitol in Williamsburg.

project required large sums of money and Jefferson sometimes ran short, paying his white workers with wheat, corn, cloth, and other goods in place of cash. His "Little Mountain" became one of the great passions of Jefferson's life, an "experiment dating back to 1619, the Burgesses demanded a traditional promise from the royal governor: he would uphold their rights to free speech and debate, protect the members' estates, and protect them from arrest while in session.

Twenty-six-year-old Jefferson gravitated toward the more radical members in the House, men like Patrick Henry. Though a newcomer to the assembly, Jefferson found himself appointed to three committees. Here he excelled at drafting legislation and resolutions. Jefferson captured and distilled ideas into forceful words. He quickly earned a reputation as a thoughtful writer and a hard worker. He wrote much—and spoke as little as possible.

Jefferson had barely settled in when the House voted on a list of resolves outlining their rights as colonists and Englishmen. They claimed that only the House of Burgesses, not Parliament, had the right to lay taxes on Virginians. They claimed their right to directly petition the king with their complaints without going to Parliament. Governor Botetourt, however, viewed the resolves with suspicion—they smacked of disloyalty. He ordered the House members into his Council Chamber at the Capitol. Jefferson filed into the room with the others and faced the governor. Botetourt told the burgesses bluntly: "You have made it my duty to dissolve you, and you are dissolved accordingly." So much for promises of free speech and debate!

When members decided to continue meeting on their own, Jefferson joined the throng crowding into the Apollo Room at the Raleigh Tavern. Here the "late representatives of the people" adopted a

Runaway

One of the great complexities of Thomas Jefferson was that he recognized slavery as an evil and even spoke against it, yet he owned hundreds of enslaved people over his lifetime and relied on their labor for his comfort and existence.

As a slave owner, Jefferson advertised in the *Virginia Gazette* in 1769 for the return of his runaway slave named Sandy. He described Sandy as about 35 years old, short and heavy, a shoemaker who'd stolen a horse, grabbed his cobbler tools, and fled. The notice claimed Sandy's "behavior is artful and knavish." Jefferson offered a reward that ended with Sandy's capture and return. Jefferson had little patience with a "knavish" runaway. He sold Sandy for a meager £10.

Jefferson did not regard Sandy as a man due liberty or choice. Yet a year later Jefferson argued in a court case that, "Under the law of nature, all men are born free. Everyone comes into the world with a right to his own person, which includes the liberty of moving and using it at his own will. This is what is called personal liberty, and [it] is given him by the Author of nature [God]." His words referred to a slave suing for his freedom. Jefferson lost the case.

RUN away from the subscriber in Albemarle, a Mulatto slave called Sandy, about 35 years of age, his stature is rather low, inclining to corpulence, and his complexion light; he is a shoemaker by trade, in which he uses his left hand principally, can do coarse carpenters work, and is something of a horse jockey; he is greatly addicted to drink, and when drunk is insolent and disorderly, in his conversation he swears much, and in his behaviour is artful and knavish. He took with him a white horse, much scarred with traces, of which it is expected he will endeavour to dispose; he also carried his shoemakers tools, and will probably endeavour to get employment that way. Whoever conveys the said slave to me, in Albemarle, shall have 40 s. reward, if taken up within the county, 4 l. if elsewhere within the colony, and 10 l. if in any other colony, from
THOMAS JEFFERSON.

Jefferson's advertisement for his runaway slave, Sandy.
COURTESY OF LIBRARY OF CONGRESS

pledge to boycott British goods. Jefferson signed his name to the document and tried to carefully follow the ban, though he slipped a few times.

SETTLING DOWN

It seems Jefferson felt little connection to his mother or siblings, except for his sister Martha, who'd married his friend, Dabney Carr. By his mid-20s, Thomas started thinking about forming a family of his own. The quest began for a suitable wife. He circulated more in Virginia society, attending the theater and social events in Williamsburg, his hair powdered in the fashion of the day, his shoe buckles gleaming in the evening candlelight.

In the spring of 1770 Martha Wayles Skelton caught his eye, a pretty young widow with a three-year-old son. No portrait of Martha survives, but people described her as petite and slender, with delicate features, large hazel eyes, and auburn hair. She also possessed a graceful manner whether on horseback or the dance floor, qualities highly prized in Virginia society. Of even greater interest to Martha's suitors—she was a wealthy woman, wealth that would belong to her new husband the moment they married.

Thomas and Martha shared much in common. She possessed a "sweetness of temper" that appealed to Jefferson. Both enjoyed talking, long walks, and reading. Best of all, Martha proved an accomplished musician, playing the harpsichord and spinet while singing in a true, sweet voice. She also displayed good sense, a great benefit for any man whose wife must run his household like a small corporation.

Captivated, Thomas emboldened his courtship to win Martha's hand, though obstacles blocked his way.

Martha and her son lived in her father's home, and John Wayles feared Thomas Jefferson was not good enough for his daughter. Jefferson had only a rough construction site to offer Martha as a home. He owned less land and fewer slaves than the men Wayles knew. And Martha, lovely, talented and wealthy, had her choice of many suitors.

Thomas often visited the Wayles home, called the Forest, bringing Martha gifts of books and a violin. He wrote his agent in England telling the man to search for a Jefferson family coat of arms in hopes that would impress John Wayles. He sped up work at Monticello so he could present Martha, whom he called Patty, a true home.

Eventually Thomas won over both Martha and her father. One family story noted that when several suitors arrived and found Thomas and Martha playing a duet on the violin and harpsichord, they shrugged and left, figuring Thomas had won Martha's heart. In February 1771 Thomas ordered from London an expensive gift of a custom-made pianoforte, his wedding present to Martha, as well as a long list of items, from a green silk umbrella to drapes and socks. But Thomas and Martha did not marry for nearly a year, perhaps because her little son died in June.

The couple married at the Forest on January 1, 1772, the bride age 23, the groom age 28. Jefferson's family attended the event. Everyone joined in as the fiddlers played robust country-dances and dined on wedding cake baked with pounds of fruit, wine, brandy, and dozens of eggs. Like many weddings in Virginia, the celebration lasted for days. The young couple left for Monticello on January 18, stopped at Tuckahoe on the way, and arrived at their own home in the middle of a blizzard. Martha set up housekeeping in the finished one-room cottage. The marriage nearly doubled Jefferson's land holdings and slaves.

At the end of September 1772 Martha gave birth to the couple's first child. They named her Martha after her mother, but called her Patsy. The pregnancy and birth, however, left delicate Martha weak and ill for months, but the baby thrived. Thomas and Martha welcomed a second daughter, named Jane, in 1774.

Jefferson did not attend sessions of the House of Burgesses from May 1771 until March 1773. He busied himself with his new family and his law practice, and managing his estates. A lover of plants and gardens, Jefferson filled over 20 new garden beds with vegetables, cultivated fruit trees, and enjoyed his flower gardens. He identified his plants with numbered sticks that he listed in his garden book, where he noted what he'd planted and how his gardens fared. He again studied Italian and devoted time to studying political ideas and science, deciding that John Locke, Sir Isaac Newton, and Francis Bacon were the three greatest men who'd ever lived.

Jefferson and Dabney Carr, a newly elected delegate, rode off to Williamsburg in March 1773 for the House session. Tensions between Great Britain and the colonies had not lessened since the Stamp

★ ACTIVITY ★
GROW A PLANT FROM A CUTTING

Jefferson propagated *(reproduced or multiplied) plants such as ornamental trees, vegetables, grasses, nut trees, and fruit trees through grafting, budding, cuttings, and growing them from seeds. New plants were tended and protected in two nurseries before they were planted in orchards or gardens.*

WHAT YOU NEED

Plant cutting from a geranium, ivy, philodendron, or other plant
Scissors or garden pruners
Glass of water
Flowerpot
Bag of potting soil

Using garden pruners or scissors, snip a 5-inch piece off of a plant such as a geranium, ivy, or philodendron. Remove any bottom leaves from your cutting stem. Root the plant by setting the stem into a glass of water. The leafy part should stay above the water.

For the next three to four weeks, keep water in the glass and observe the stem. You should see tiny, hairlike roots begin to develop off the stem. After the roots grow thicker and longer, it is time to transplant the cutting into a pot.

If your pot does not have a drain hole, place rocks or packing peanuts in the bottom. Add potting soil. Stick the rooted stem into the potting soil. With your fingers, firm the soil around the root. Water your new plant, give it sunlight, and watch it grow. You have made a new plant from an old one!

Act repeal of 1766. Instead, Britain passed more taxes and colonists protested with mob violence and boycotts. In 1768 the king sent 4,000 red-coated soldiers to control the rabble-rousers of Boston, a hot spot of mob "mischief." On a March day in 1770, a handful of frightened soldiers fired into a mob of nearly 400 people, killing five men. The *Boston Gazette* blamed the tragedy—the "Boston Massacre"—on "quartering troops among citizens in a time of peace."

Jefferson feared Parliament's growing power over the colonies. Many burgesses arrived in no mood to work with the royal governor. Indeed, Governor Dunmore had only called the House into session because he needed tax money. Along with Carr, Jefferson helped set up the Committees of Correspondence, a network of letter writers in the colonies to "obtain the most early and authentic" news of Parliament's actions.

But working in the House of Burgesses with his friend and brother-in-law proved short-lived. Dabney Carr died in May 1773, leaving his wife and six children. Jefferson buried his friend at Monticello. Martha Carr and the children lived off and on with her brother's family at Monticello.

Only a few weeks later John Wayles died. Martha inherited 11,000 acres and 135 slaves from her father. The inheritance, which became Jefferson's property, made him one of the largest slave owners in Virginia, with 169 slaves. While Martha's inheritance made Jefferson rich, he also had to settle John Wayles's £4,000 of debt. Jefferson was no stranger to debt, which never stopped him from splurging on further

The *"Boston Massacre."*
COURTESY OF LIBRARY OF CONGRESS

luxuries. As a member of the Virginia aristocracy and a gentleman, Jefferson had to display certain standards of ease and wealth or the neighbors might gossip about his decayed fortunes.

His debt and the British Parliament were not the only items frustrating Jefferson. He became increasingly frustrated with the legal world—lawyers, judges, the court systems, and wringing payment from his clients. In summer 1774 he retired from law and turned over his cases to one of his Randolph cousins. He would live as a gentleman planter, and with more free time, he turned his focus to politics.

"JUSTICE WITH A HEAVY HAND INDEED!"

The spring and summer of 1774 proved a time of anxiety throughout the colonies. A British tax on tea had led dozens of men to board British ships in December 1773 and dump 342 chests of expensive tea leaves into Boston Harbor.

King George and Parliament reacted with fury. British warships blocked the port of Boston, forcing the town's citizens to face ruin and starvation. People arrested for crimes would be transported to England for trial. All Massachusetts officials, judges, and sheriffs would be appointed by the new royal governor and answer directly to the king, not the elected colonial assembly. The governor also banned town meetings and canceled the fall elections for the assembly.

Demonstrations against these Coercive Acts, called "Intolerable Acts" in the colonies, erupted in towns across America. The Committees of Correspondence plied their pens with news and solidarity for Boston's suffering. "This is administering justice with a heavy hand indeed!" wrote an appalled Jefferson.

He probably drafted the resolution passed by the Virginia Assembly calling for "a day of fasting, humiliation, and prayer" on June 1 in support of Boston. Virginians would be of "one heart and one

The Hemings Family

Betty Hemings and her 11 children became the property of Thomas Jefferson on the death of John Wayles. Martha Jefferson had grown up with the Hemingses. Most likely, some of Betty's children were the half siblings of Martha Jefferson. Over the decades Thomas Jefferson held more than 80 people related to Betty Hemings in bondage.

The Hemings family held a place above all other slaves at Monticello. Jefferson valued the family's loyalty, while many of the Hemingses mastered skills and trades that made them even more valuable to Jefferson. The family did not have to work in the fields, even for the yearly cutting and stacking of wheat when Jefferson called on all his slaves to help. Betty's sons, John and James, could hire themselves out for pay when Jefferson didn't need them. Betty and her children received clothing sewn from soft muslin, Irish linen, and calico far better than the rough woven cloth issued to other slaves. Jefferson paid two members of the Hemings clan, John Hemings and nephew Burwell Colbert, a yearly bonus for their good and faithful work.

The greatest prize—freedom—was granted to only 11 slaves at Monticello out of the 600 men and women Jefferson owned over his lifetime. All 11 were the children or grandchildren of Betty Hemings.

mind firmly to oppose . . . every injury to American rights." The resolution called Britain's act a "hostile invasion" of "our sister colony." Once more Governor Dunmore rebuked the troublesome House members and Jefferson noted, "The Governor dissolved us as usual." Again members trekked down Duke of Gloucester Street to the Raleigh Tavern.

Everyone wondered which town or colony would next feel the crown's wrath. Jefferson sent letters calling other House members back to Williamsburg, even though they met without authority. "Things seem to be hurrying to an alarming crisis," he wrote, "and demand the speedy, united counsel of all those who have a regard for the common cause."

RIGHTS OF BRITISH AMERICA

The colonies agreed to send delegates for a meeting in Philadelphia. This Continental Congress would decide how best to deal with the Intolerable Acts. Jefferson drafted instructions for the Virginia delegates detailing a list of faults for both king and Parliament. Jefferson urged the king to "let no act be passed by any one legislature which may infringe on the right and liberties of another." He argued against each liberty-crushing act passed by Parliament to punish Massachusetts, writing in part that, "his majesty has no right to land a single armed man on our shores . . . let him remember that force cannot give right."

Jefferson also claimed George III and Parliament had "invaded the natural and legal rights" of Americans, trampling long-standing laws. The colonies, he claimed, since their founding were only "subject to the laws which they had adopted at their first settlement" or any laws accepted by their own legislatures. He brashly summed up:

> These are our grievances, which we have thus laid before his Majesty, with that freedom of language and sentiment which becomes a free people, claiming their rights as derived from the laws of nature, and not as the gift of their chief magistrate. . . . Kings are the servants,

King George III of Great Britain.
COURTESY OF LIBRARY OF CONGRESS

not the proprietors of the people. Open your breast, Sire, to liberal and expanded thought. Let not the name of George the third be a blot on the page of history.

With Jefferson too sick to attend the debate over his instructions, other House members toned down his views in the final directions to the delegates. Some friends, however, had 200 copies of Jefferson's draft printed in August 1774 as *A Summary View of the Rights of British America.* The pamphlet spread rapidly, read throughout the colonies and as far away as London. *A Summary View* established Jefferson's reputation as a skilled writer—and a man with radical ideas.

On October 1, 1774, the First Continental Congress sent King George III a Declaration of Colonial Rights and Grievances. British liberties had been denied them, liberties such as the right of representation and the right to gather and petition the king. They asked for a repeal of tax acts. They urged the king to withdraw troops in Boston brought in peacetime without the peoples' consent. And they passed the Continental Association—another boycott on British goods. But Jefferson, back in Virginia, wished for bolder words and stronger measures.

Meanwhile, he immersed himself in Monticello and his little family. He revised his plans for the house, adding more rooms for a total of eight. Finishing work continued on the parlor, library, drawing room, and master bedroom. He gardened, planned a winemaking business, and bought and sold land.

Gloomy news arrived from Britain. George III announced his determination to uphold the "supreme authority" of Parliament. The king ignored the petition from the Continental Congress. In March 1775 Jefferson attended the Virginia Convention in Richmond, free from the controlling hands of Governor Dunmore in Williamsburg. On March 23, 1775, Patrick Henry warned the convention that Virginia needed to prepare for armed conflict. A second Continental Congress in Philadelphia was planned for spring of 1775. Jefferson was eventually selected to replace his ailing relative Peyton Randolph as a delegate.

It seemed one crisis after another rolled over the colonies. In early May, Thomas wrote William Small about the skirmishes at Lexington and Concord, which left 49 Americans and 73 British soldiers dead. "Within this week we have received the unhappy news of an action of considerable magnitude, between the King's troops and our breathren of Boston," Thomas wrote. "This accident has cut off our last hope of reconciliation, and a phrensy of revenge seems to have seized all ranks of people."

In mid-June 1775 Jefferson left Virginia for the Second Continental Congress. He traveled by coach, attended by several slaves, including Jupiter. He arrived in Philadelphia greeted by harrowing news from Massachusetts of the June 17 battle fought on Breed's Hill. At the end of the day more than 1,000 men lay dead on the bloody slopes while below, the city of Charlestown burned. Just a few days earlier Congress had voted to raise six companies of soldiers and named George Washington the commander in chief of all Continental forces. Now militias from around New England poured into Boston.

Jefferson rented rooms with cabinetmaker Benjamin Randolph on Chestnut Street. Jefferson designed a folding writing box that opened into a desk, complete with a drawer, and Randolph built the desk to his order. He also bought a new chair and hired a barber to come round and shave him at his room. Thus settled in, he prepared for work.

MAKE FRESH GRAPE JUICE

For years Jefferson tried unsuccessfully to grow grapes for a Monticello wine, but disease attacked European grapevines and American grapes lacked the right flavor. Since you can't drink wine, try some fresh grape juice, instead!

ADULT SUPERVISION REQUIRED

WHAT YOU NEED

Grapes (about 7 pounds of grapes make 8 cups of juice, or 1 pound of grapes makes a bit less than a cup of juice)

Large stockpot (12 quarts)

Potato masher

Fine mesh sieve or cheesecloth

Large pot (6 to 8 quarts)

Kitchen twine, or rubber band if using cheesecloth

Ladle

Wash the grapes under running water. Pick them off the stems and put them into the larger pot. Toss out any shriveled or unripe grapes.

Using a potato masher, mash the grapes until the juice starts flowing. You may have to mash some of the grapes, then mash another batch.

With an adult's supervision, bring the pot of mashed grapes

to a simmer (barely bubbling) on a stove. Simmer for five minutes, stirring occasionally. Mash the grapes even more, breaking up the grapes as much as you can, then simmer for five more minutes.

Put a fine mesh sieve or two layers of cheesecloth secured with twine or a rubber band over the second pot. Set the pot on a large plate to catch any overflow. Ladle the cooled grape mixture over the sieve or cheesecloth to strain. Let the pot, sieve, and plate sit overnight in the refrigerator to strain all the juice.

In the morning, if using cheesecloth, fold the cheese-cloth over any grape skins and squeeze out any extra juice. Rinse out the sieve or cheesecloth and strain the juice again to filter out any sediment. Pour or ladle juice into a pitcher or cup and enjoy your freshly made grape juice!

Several delegates noted Jefferson's arrival. Governor Samuel Ward wrote his brother, "Yesterday the famous Mr. Jefferson arrived. I have not been in company with him yet. He looks like a very sensible spirited fine fellow and by the pamphlet which he wrote last summer, he certainly is one." John Adams of Massachusetts, a brilliant legal mind, commented on Jefferson's "happy talent for composition." He soon noted that Jefferson disliked speaking in front of Congress and kept mostly silent, but in committee work Jefferson was "prompt, frank, explicit, and decisive." Shy and often withdrawn, Jefferson preferred working alone, distanced from the bickering and debates of Congress.

Congress put Thomas's talent for composition to steady work over the next few months as he drafted papers and wrote resolutions. For one address he modified his ideas from *A Summary View of the Rights of British America* into a paper called "A Declaration of the Causes & Necessity for Taking Up Arms." He calculated the cost of war with Great Britain, figuring a six-month conflict would cost around $3 million.

Jefferson's views differed from those of more conservative delegates like John Dickinson, a Philadelphia lawyer. These men still hoped Great Britain would snap to her senses and recognize the rights of the colonies. William Livingston of New Jersey described the heated language used by some "Southern gentlemen" versus the more cool rhetoric of the moderates. One draft document "had faults common to our Southern gentlemen. Much fault-finding and declamation, with little sense or dignity.

The Pennsylvania State House.
COURTESY OF LIBRARY OF CONGRESS

They seem to think a reiteration of [the words] tyranny, despotism, bloody, etc., all that is needed to unite us."

Jefferson got along much better with like-minded men, such as Benjamin Franklin and John Adams. Adams warned that moderate and conservative delegates must be converted slowly to the more radical side.

Some evenings Thomas mingled at Smith's City Tavern with other delegates. He browsed Philadelphia's shops, snapping up books and sheets of music to take home. But the delegates enjoyed little freedom for such diversions. Congress met from nine to five each day with committee work in the early mornings or evenings. They worked in the assembly chamber of the Pennsylvania State House, the windows shut against loyalist ears, so that droning flies instead of warm breezes punctuated the debates.

With General Washington at Cambridge and the British hunkered down in Boston, weary delegates must have glanced at one another and wondered what would happen next. On July 5, 1775, Congress approved John Dickinson's proposal for an Olive Branch Petition to the king. The petition blamed British officials for forcing the colonies "to arm in our own defense" and claimed that most Americans desired harmony with Great Britain. They asked George III to grant the colonies relief.

In August Jefferson left Philadelphia for Virginia. He collected Martha, Patsy, and Jane from the Forest where they'd gone to stay with Martha's sister and brother-in-law, Elizabeth and Francis Eppes. The family gathered again at Monticello only to meet tragedy when 17-month-old Jane died.

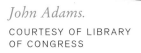

John Adams.
COURTESY OF LIBRARY OF CONGRESS

COMMON SENSE

Personal sadness and politics weighed on Jefferson. He wrote his cousin John Randolph, who'd soon leave for England, that, "Even those in Parliament who are called friends to America, seem to know nothing of our real determination." Jefferson admitted that if America must be dependent on another nation, he would "rather be in dependence on Great Britain, properly limited, than on any other nation on earth." But, since the British Parliament had shown "they will so cruelly exercise" the right of legislating for us, he "would lend my hand to sink the whole island in the ocean." Meanwhile Jefferson hoped for the "returning wisdom of Great Britain" and his own wish to "withdraw myself totally from the public stage."

But instead of withdrawal, Jefferson returned to Philadelphia in October. He plunged into work, serving on the Committee on Currency (money), the Committee on the Business of Congress, and committees on petitions and disputes. The delegates learned that George III ignored their Olive Branch Petition and instead declared the colonies in a state of rebellion. The royal proclamation, dated August 1775 announced:

> Whereas many of our subjects ... of our Colonies in North America, misled by dangerous ... men, and forgetting the allegiance which they owe to the power that has protected and supported them ... have ... proceeded to open ... rebellion ... traitorously preparing ... war against us.

Rumors that Governor Dunmore requested British warships in Virginia alarmed Jefferson with fear for his family. Dunmore also made an empty promise of freedom to any slaves belonging to rebels, provided the slaves ran away to fight for the king. Jefferson sent a frantic letter to his brother-in-law Francis Eppes. "I have never received the script of a pen from any mortal in Virginia since I left it, nor been able by any inquiries I could make to hear of my family.... The suspense under which I am is too terrible to be endured. If anything has happened, for God's sake, let me know."

December 1775 brought coastal skirmishes between Dunmore's British soldiers and the new Virginia regiment. Unable to bear being away from his family in uncertain and dangerous times, Thomas left Congress, picked up Martha and Patsy at the Forest, and returned to Monticello. For the next four months he holed up at home. In March 1776 his mother died suddenly. Most troubling, Martha's health remained fragile, and for five weeks in the spring Thomas suffered such severe migraine headaches he could not crawl out of bed.

Thomas Nelson, a fellow congressman, urged Jefferson to return to Philadelphia and bring Martha with him. "Mrs. Nelson shall nurse her and take all possible care of her," he offered. Nelson also sent Jefferson a copy of a new hot-selling pamphlet by Thomas Paine, published in January 1776, titled *Common Sense*.

In 47 pages Paine argued against every reason to remain under Britain's wing. Instead, wrote Paine, the colonies would flourish without England's clutching hands. Then he championed and made crystal clear an idea that Thomas Jefferson had already started to believe. In place of a corrupt

A 1775 British cartoon shows a Virginia loyalist forced to sign a document by a Williamsburg mob while tar and feathers hang in the background.
COURTESY OF LIBRARY OF CONGRESS

king, asked Paine, why not say that in America "THE LAW IS KING." "O ye that love mankind! Ye that dare oppose not only the tyranny, but the tyrant, stand forth!" proclaimed Paine. Let all Americans become "supporter[s] of the RIGHTS OF MANKIND, and of the FREE AND INDEPENDENT STATES OF AMERICA."

★ CHAPTER ★ 3

"In Open Rebellion"

The small crack that once divided Great Britain and her colonies now yawned like a giant chasm. The British fleet, carrying thousands of soldiers and fleeing loyalists, sailed from Boston. Many feared New York loomed as the next British target. Washington knew the British outmanned, outgunned, and outsupplied his army at every turn. Many Americans could simply not believe how swiftly events unraveled. How had it gone from questioning how much obedience "we owe to the British Parliament" to "whether we are members of the empire or not," a New Yorker confided to his journal. In the coming weeks Americans faced a weighty decision: where did their loyalties truly lie?

A reconstruction of the Graff House, where Jefferson wrote the Declaration of Independence.
COURTESY OF INDEPENDENCE NATIONAL HISTORICAL PARK

Thomas Jefferson, arriving back in Philadelphia on May 14, 1776, knew he was one of those the king labeled "in open rebellion." He rented new rooms in the house of German bricklayer Jacob Graff and set up his desk and chair, ready for business. Congress had just passed John Adams's resolution advising the colonies to write new constitutions for independent state governments. Some of Jefferson's former fellow delegates remained in Virginia to attend the state Constitutional Convention.

In the House of Burgesses, all members voted "aye" to resolves meant for the delegates in Philadelphia. The resolves called for a motion in the Continental Congress to dissolve "all allegiance to or dependence upon the Crown or Parliament of Great Britain." Then they pulled down the British flag from atop the Capitol and hoisted a new banner to flutter above the city—a flag representing the Continental Union.

Jefferson wished he too had stayed in Virginia, contributing to his state's new constitution. "It is a work of the most interesting nature," he wrote a friend in Williamsburg, "and such as every individual would wish to have a voice in. In truth, it is the whole object of the present controversy."

As May passed and the weeks ticked by in June, Jefferson scribbled drafts of a constitution for Virginia. He proposed an elected assembly, a senate chosen from the assembly members, and a governor who did little but paperwork and served a one-year term. He would grant every white male 50 acres of land from Virginia's vast acres, making that man a property owner, and therefore eligible to vote. His writings reached Virginia too late for the convention to consider.

On June 7, 1776, Richard Henry Lee, acting on the instructions from the House of Burgesses, stood before the gathered Congress. Everyone in the Assembly Room of the Pennsylvania State House knew what was coming. Jefferson listened from his usual chair near the fireplace. Lee spoke the words long awaited by some, long dreaded by others: "These united colonies are, and of right ought to be, free and independent states. They are absolved [released] from all allegiance to the British Crown, and that all political connection between them . . . is, and ought to be, totally dissolved."

John Adams leapt to his feet to approve the proposal. The questions of independence, so monumental, so important, charged the chamber like a bolt of lightning. Conservative delegates urged restraint—the colonies must not jump into the dangerous unknown of independence. Delegates from New York and New Jersey could take no action without instructions from their state assemblies. Congress agreed to postpone further debate until July 1 and appointed a committee to draft a declaration of independence for consideration. The job fell to Adams, Benjamin Franklin, Roger Sherman, Robert Livingston, and Thomas Jefferson.

"WE HOLD THESE TRUTHS"

Years later John Adams recalled, "Mr. Jefferson desired me to . . . make the Draught [draft]." But Adams said, no, Jefferson should write the draft instead. Adams rammed his point home with several arguments. Jefferson was from Virginia, the most populous and oldest colony, and Virginia had sent the resolves for independence that Lee proposed. Adams claimed he himself was "so obnoxious for my early and constant Zeal" in promoting independence that his draft would be viewed with "severe Scrutiny and Criticism." Last of all, urged Adams, he had great respect for "the elegance" of Jefferson's

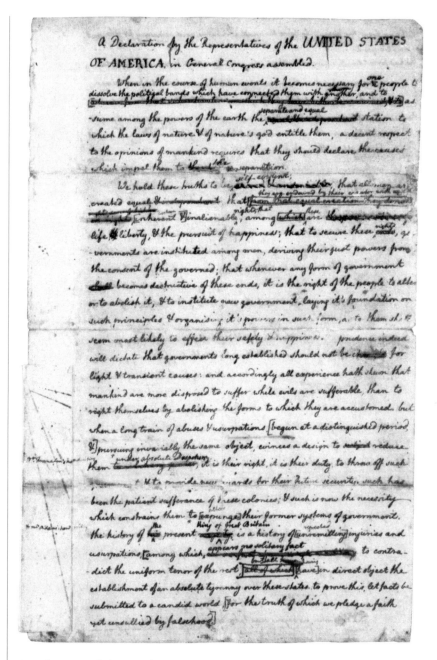

Draft copy of the Declaration of Independence.
COURTESY OF LIBRARY OF CONGRESS

Jefferson has Adams and Franklin review his draft.
COURTESY OF LIBRARY OF CONGRESS

pen "and none at all of my own." Jefferson agreed to do the job, though 47 years later he remembered events differently. The job was "unanimously pressed on myself alone to undertake the draught. I consented; I drew it."

So 33-year-old Jefferson wrote a declaration of independence for Congress to debate. At the same time he spent late nights tinkering on versions of a constitution for Virginia. He viewed his new assignment from Congress like any other report or resolve he drafted while sitting on committees. And it was the committee that would present the draft to Congress. For several years, no one would really know Thomas Jefferson wrote the eloquent statement of independence.

Jefferson's new quarters lay only a short walk from the state house and his two rooms on the second floor offered "freely circulating air" in the muggy summer heat. He worked early morning and at night at his portable folding desk, his quill pen scratching across the surface of his paper. He sipped tea and ate biscuits. As he wrote, revised, and polished, carefully weighing each word like a lawyer preparing an important case, Jefferson distilled all his years of studying, reading, and thinking into his draft.

"The history of the present King of Great Britain," wrote Jefferson, "is a History of . . . injuries & usurpations . . . all have in direct object the establishment of an absolute tyranny over these States. To prove this, let facts be submitted to a candid world." Jefferson then laid out 27 charges against the king. He had no doubt the colonies

Delegates debated the Declaration of Independence in the Assembly Room of the Pennsylvania State House.
COURTESY OF INDEPENDENCE NATIONAL HISTORICAL PARK, PHOTO BY ROBIN MILLER

would accept independence, but he must have wondered if he'd end up dangling from a tree, hanged as a traitor.

Thomas wrote the draft over the next two weeks, passing it on to Adams and Franklin for comments. On June 28 the committee presented the document titled "A Declaration by the Representatives in General Congress Assembled" to the other members. Outside the tall windows storm clouds gathered, the day muggy, the men inside the steamy chamber sweating as debate on the weighty issue began. Anxious men faced one another, arguing, pleading, tempers flaring.

John Dickinson of Pennsylvania spoke eloquently for the more conservative members. "Shall we destroy, in a moment of anger" the bonds and loyalties "cemented and tested by time?" he asked. It was too soon for such a tremendous step—

If Americans at the time paid more attention to the crimes laid at the feet of George III in the Declaration of Independence, later generations remembered Jefferson's earlier passages. In a few short words, Jefferson gave voice to the Enlightenment, summed up the ideals of America, and created the shining legacy of the American Revolution.

> We hold these Truths to be self-evident, that all Men are created equal, that they are endowed by their Creator with certain unalienable Rights, that among these are Life, Liberty, and the Pursuit of Happiness—That to secure these Rights, Governments are instituted among Men, deriving their just Powers from the Consent of the Governed, that whenever any Form of Government becomes destructive of these Ends, it is the Right of the People to alter or abolish it, and to institute new Government.

Great Britain too strong, the colonies too weak. What would they accomplish by such a headstrong response? Declaring independence, warned Dickinson, would be like destroying their homes in winter before they had built another safe shelter.

Proud of his work on the draft, Jefferson slumped in his chair next to Ben Franklin, fuming in silence as Congress toiled line by line through his writing, striking out sentences and sections, and adding changes. Congress's editing actually sharpened and focused some of Jefferson's arguments, but the editing proved difficult for Jefferson to endure.

The greatest controversy arose from Jefferson's passage holding George III responsible for the continuation of slavery and the slave trade in the colonies. This made little sense, as slavery had existed long before the king came to power and the colonies actively took part in the slave trade and in owning slaves. Jefferson owned slaves and his enslaved servant, Bob Hemings, attended him in Philadelphia. Congress marked through this section where Jefferson condemned slavery as "a cruel war against human nature itself."

As the day dragged on a terrific storm battered against the windows, reflecting the turmoil inside the chamber. That night, with tempers frayed, the delegates took a test vote. Nine states voted in favor of independence. South Carolina and Pennsylvania opposed the measure. Delaware's delegates stood divided and New York's delegates still awaited instructions. Congress postponed the debate until the next day, July 2.

Tradition claims that John Hancock, president of the Congress, addressed the delegates. "We must be unanimous," he urged, "there must be no pulling different ways, we must all hang together." To this Benjamin Franklin observed, "Yes; we must indeed hang together, or, most assuredly we shall all hang separately!" They knew the vote must be unanimous on this great issue. A vote for independence not only meant all-out war against the might of Great Britain but would also brand each man in the chamber a traitor.

Events shifted on July 2. Caesar Rodney of Delaware, dying of cancer, rode through the night to cast his vote for independence. South Carolina switched to yes. John Dickinson and Robert Morris

CREATE A DECLARATION OF INDEPENDENCE WORD SEARCH

WHAT YOU NEED

Ruler

Graph paper

Pencil with an eraser

Copy of the Declaration of Independence
(look online)

Marker

Using the ruler, draw a square (size of your choosing) on graph paper. The smaller the square, the smaller the puzzle and the fewer words you will use.

Select words from Thomas Jefferson's Declaration of Independence. Write as many words as you want on the graph paper inside the drawn square, putting one letter in each of the graph paper's little squares. Use capital letters. Words can go across, up and down, backward, and diagonally.

To the side, keep a list of the words you are using. Players will use the list to know what to look for.

After you have written in the words of your choice, fill in all the extra squares with random letters. To be tricky, use short letter combinations that are *part* of some of the words you used. Let friends and family try your puzzle. They should circle or highlight with a marker the words they find.

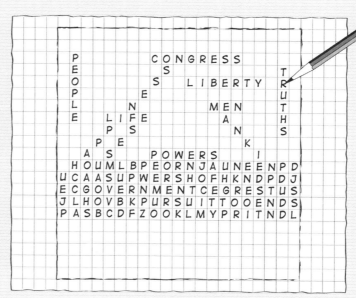

CONGRESS
LIBERTY
TRUTHS
MANKIND
POWERS
SAFETY
HAPPINESS
LIFE
GOVERNMENT
PEOPLE
CAUSES
MEN
PURSUIT

Detail from John Trumbull painting of the committee presenting the Declaration to Congress.
COURTESY OF LIBRARY OF CONGRESS

of Pennsylvania, who could not in good conscience vote for independence, chose not to vote at all. The remaining Pennsylvania delegates voted yes. New York still abstained. So in the end, on July 2, 1776, the resolution presented by Lee of Virginia passed—the colonies declared independence from Great Britain. John Adams, who'd labored mightily for this moment, wrote his wife Abigail, "Yesterday the greatest Question was decided."

On July 4, Congress formally approved the final version of the document. John Dunlap of Philadelphia printed the first copies of the Declaration of Independence. Four days later crowds gathered in Philadelphia to hear Jefferson's words read aloud. Meanwhile, riders galloped north and south with the news. On July 9, in New York, George Washington had the Declaration of Independence read to his soldiers. Everything had now changed; the birth of a new nation lay at stake.

Jefferson objected to many of the changes in his draft. He'd felt humiliated by the debate over his work. Later that summer, he copied out his *original* draft, with edited sections restored and Congress's 86 changes, both large and small, banished to the margins. He sent this version to his friends, not the "mangled" version printed in Philadelphia. Decades later, as an old man writing his autobiography, Jefferson included the entire "form of the Declaration as originally reported" with "the parts struck out by Congress" underlined in black. The wounds of July 1776 still stung!

HOME TO VIRGINIA

News from Virginia twisted Thomas with anxiety. George Wythe wrote of his misgivings about the new Virginia state constitution. Fears for Martha, who might have suffered a miscarriage, tortured Thomas. He wrote Richard Henry Lee, back in Virginia, to rush to Philadelphia and take his place. "For God's sake, for your country's sake and for my sake, come," Thomas wrote at the end of July. "I am under a sacred obligation to go home." His term in Congress expired in August and he frantically wrote his friends not to vote him another term. He plugged away on his committee work, and when Lee arrived in Philadelphia on September 3, Thomas hastily bought clothes and treats for his wife and daughter then scurried home in record time—only six days!

Three weeks after his return to Monticello, state business called Jefferson to Williamsburg. This time Martha and Patsy, along with baggage wagons and servants, made the 150-mile trip with him. They moved into George Wythe's house as Jefferson prepared to serve in the new Virginia House of Delegates.

The day after they arrived, he received an urgent message from John Hancock: Jefferson had been appointed to join Benjamin Franklin and Silas Deane as a commissioner to the court of King Louis XVI of France. A ship waited to carry Jefferson and his family on the first leg of their journey to Paris. But Martha's health prevented her from making the exhausting trip. For three days Jefferson struggled, undecided, keeping the messenger waiting. On October 11, he turned down the opportunity due to "circumstances very peculiar in the situation of my family."

Jefferson made a new friend and staunch political ally in James Madison, a friendship that spanned the next five decades. In the spring of 1777 he began a correspondence with John Adams, sealing the bond forged as allies at the Continental Congress. He also shared letters with numerous friends, touching on subjects of politics, music, and science. To Italian Giovanni Fabbroni he wrote how he loved and envied Italy's music. "This is the favorite passion of my soul, & Fortune has cast my lot in a country where it is in a state of deplorable barbarism." To scientist David Rittenhouse, Jefferson exclaimed, "The amazing mechanical representation of the solar system which you conceived &

BUILD A MODEL SOLAR SYSTEM

Among Jefferson's scientific instruments was an "orrery and planetarium" purchased in 1790. This mechanical, movable model of the solar system highlighted Enlightenment thinking—the universe worked in a rational order based on nature's laws. In Jefferson's time the planet Neptune had not yet been discovered (that happened in 1846). You can include Neptune or leave it off.

ADULT SUPERVISION REQUIRED

WHAT YOU NEED

2 wooden dowel rods, 36 inches by ⅛ inch

Small handsaw

Paintbrush

Acrylic paints: bright yellow, bright red, light blue, deep blue, burnt orange, coral, terra-cotta, purple, green, black

Styrofoam sheet, 12 inches by 36 inches

Drawing compass

6-inch square of cardboard

Pencil

Tacky glue

1 Styrofoam ball, 6-inch diameter

3 Styrofoam balls, 1½-inch diameter

1 Styrofoam ball, 1-inch diameter

2 Styrofoam balls, 2-inch diameter

1 Styrofoam ball, 4-inch diameter

1 Styrofoam ball, 3-inch diameter

Ruler

4½-inch Styrofoam ring

Rubber band

Using a small handsaw, cut the dowel rods into pieces of these lengths: 2½, 4, 5, 6, 7, 8, 10, 11½ inches. Paint the pieces black and stick them in a Styrofoam sheet to dry.

Make Saturn's ring. Use a drawing compass to make a 3-inch circle on the cardboard or hold the 3-inch ball on the cardboard. Lay your pencil against the fattest part of the ball and trace a circle onto the cardboard. Now make a second circle of 5½-inch diameter around the 3-inch circle. Cut out the center to fit around the 3-inch ball.

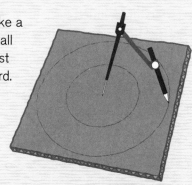

Glue the dowels into the Styrofoam balls following this guide:

- 4-inch ball: 7-inch dowel

- 3-inch ball: 8-inch dowel

- 1-inch ball: 2½-inch dowel

- First 1½-inch ball: 4-inch dowel

- Second 1½-inch ball: 5-inch dowel

- Third 1½-inch ball: 6-inch dowel

- First 2-inch ball: 10-inch dowel

- Second 2-inch ball: 11½-inch dowel

Follow the colors below or look up photos of the planets for their colors. If two colors are used, paint the first color, then dab on the second color:

- 6-inch ball (the sun): bright yellow

- 1-inch ball (Mercury): deep blue

- 1½-inch ball with shortest dowel (Venus): burnt orange with coral

- 1½-inch ball with medium-size dowel (Earth): deep blue with green

- 1½-inch ball with longest dowel (Mars): burnt orange

- 4-inch ball (Jupiter): coral with terra-cotta rings

- 3-inch ball with ring (Saturn): terra-cotta, paint rings around the ball

- 2-inch ball with shorter dowel (Uranus): deep blue

- 2-inch ball with longer dowel (Neptune): light blue.

Paint the Styrofoam ring black. When everything is dry, glue the sun to the black ring, which will serve as the base of your model.

Put a rubber band around the sun, about 2½ inches above the base. Glue the planets into the sun below the rubber band. Start with Mercury, the closest to the sun, then move around the sun placing the others. Take the rubber band off when the planets are attached.

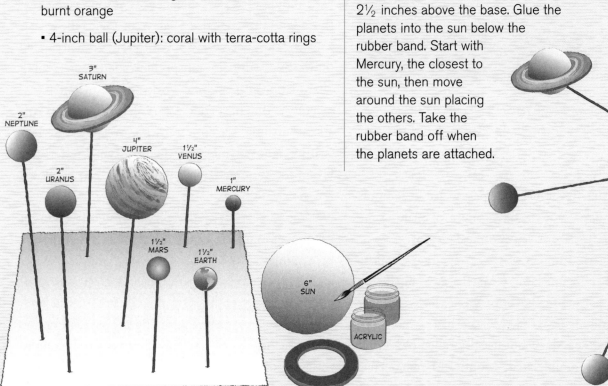

James Madison, whose friendship and political alliance with Jefferson spanned five decades.
COURTESY OF LIBRARY OF CONGRESS

executed, has never been surpassed." He reminds Rittenhouse "of your kind promise of making me an accurate clock" for astronomical purposes.

In the early summer of 1777, tragedy once more visited the Jefferson family. Martha gave birth to a baby boy who survived only three weeks. A year later on August 1, 1778, Martha had a daughter. They named her Mary, but usually called her Maria or Polly. This child lived. Monticello remained a construction site and Jefferson planted fruit trees in his south orchard, rows of cherry, apple, pear, plum, apricot, and almond trees.

LAWS AND REFORM

Jefferson's depth of legal knowledge, his ability to create order and make complex issues clear, seemed a perfect match for his newest assignment. The legislature appointed Jefferson head of a committee to revise, change, and trim the entire code of Virginia law. Jefferson aimed to streamline Virginia's court system, opening the courts more often to avoid a backlog of cases. He wanted to simplify and shorten the legal codes. He also sought more humane punishments. He hoped criminals might be reformed and executions used only as "the last melancholy resource" against those who threatened the safety of their fellow citizens. At the time nearly 300 different crimes carried the death penalty. For most offenses Jefferson favored "hard labor in the public works" as punishment.

Over the next few years Jefferson proposed an astonishing 126 new reforms or laws. The legislature ignored most of them, leaving Jefferson's vision for Virginia largely untouched. But he won a few successes.

In one proposal Jefferson advocated freedom of religion in Virginia. Jefferson viewed religion as a private matter and believed in religious liberty for all. He also wanted separation of the state government from any control by the Church of England, now known in America as the Episcopal Church. As it stood, Virginia compelled all citizens to belong to the Episcopal Church and to support it with taxes, even if people personally held different beliefs.

Jefferson filled his pockets with an assortment of miniature tools for observing, measuring, and record-ing the world around him, what he called his "traveling calculator." He also carried an "ivory note-book," small bound finger-length pieces of ivory, where he scribbled notes in pencil. At the end of the day he transferred his notes into one of his record books for his farms, his gardens, and his finances, and then erased the notes written on his ivory notebook.

WHAT YOU NEED

Sheets of stiff card stock, about $\frac{1}{16}$ inch thick

Ruler

Pencil

Scissors

Hole punch

A ring, such as a key chain

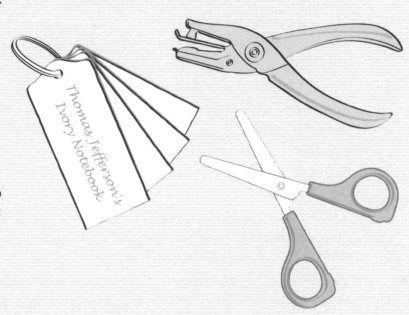

On card stock, draw the outline of your "page," about 3½ inches long and 1½ inches wide.

Cut out the shape with scissors. Use the shape to trace other pages and cut them out. You will want five or six pages.

Punch holes at one end of the pages. Slip each page onto your key chain. Now you have a handy way to take notes just like Jefferson.

Jefferson rarely attended church. The strict practices and rituals of the church rubbed against his sense of individual freedom of thought. Jefferson had read religious philosophy since his youth. He believed in a supreme being who created the universe, established laws to run it, then stepped back allowing events to unfurl. Jefferson's Statute for Religious Freedom did pass, but not until January 1786.

One reform dear to Jefferson, which never gathered much support, was establishing a system of free public schools in Virginia. Jefferson called his plan the Bill for the General Diffusion of Knowledge, the cornerstone of "a crusade against ignorance." Jefferson wanted all white male children to have three years of free education in local "ward" schools. From there select boys moved on to a county school, and the very brightest advanced to college. Jefferson envisioned a new "aristocracy of virtue and talent" where educated citizens protected their republic and their liberties.

GOVERNOR JEFFERSON

The war raged north and south, but Jefferson mostly tended his garden, played his violin, kept track of the daily weather, and worked on the immense code of laws. Sick of politics, he longed to retreat permanently into his home, his gardens, his family, and his studies. "You are too young," Edmund Pendleton chided him, "to ask that happy quietus from the public life."

Jefferson voted to supply and raise troops for Washington's army and to seize loyalist property. When 5,000 German Hessians—soldiers rented out by their ruler to George III—arrived in Albemarle County as prisoners of war, Jefferson oversaw the building of barracks and gathering of food. Jefferson even entertained Hessian officers at Monticello, where he and Martha provided books, food, and music.

In June 1779 the Virginia House elected Jefferson to a one-year term as governor of Virginia. Jefferson once again uprooted his family, this time moving into the Governor's Palace in Williamsburg. The governor had no real power—not like the royal governors—thanks in part to Jefferson's own efforts. As governor he could not veto a law, dissolve the assembly, appoint men to offices, grant pardons, or call out the militia without assembly approval. He also needed approval from a new Council of State, which included good friends John Page and James Madison, but seldom had enough members present to act.

Jefferson governed over the new nation's largest state with a population of around 500,000 white citizens and roughly the same number of enslaved people. British warships loomed offshore, occasionally sailing inland from the Chesapeake Bay to destroy stores of tobacco and raid towns.

Virginia's economy, like the economy of the United States, lay in ruins. People would not or could not pay taxes to support the states, so the states printed sheaves of paper money, which soon had little value at all. Jefferson sought new business for Virginia, encouraging cloth weaving, leather tanning, and gunpowder and weapons manufacturing. He tried to raise money by confiscating loyalists' lands and selling tracts of western lands, but nothing much helped. Meanwhile, from Congress in

Philadelphia arrived a steady stream of demands for money, uniforms, and more soldiers. But Jefferson usually had only empty hands to offer. The war continued badly, the United States suffering defeats in battle, the army undermanned and unpaid, and the economy crashing.

In April 1780 Jefferson moved Virginia's capital from the old colonial seat at Williamsburg to Richmond, a town of about 1,800 people. The new capital's location seemed safer from the British fleet. Jefferson envisioned grand plans for the capital city, plans he lovingly labored over for the next decade. He rented a brick house overlooking the Great Falls of the James River and moved in his family along with 49 crates of books, wine, paintings, furniture, china, chandeliers, and government records.

On November 30, 1780, Martha gave birth to another daughter, named Lucy Elizabeth. Martha's poor health, due to difficulties with pregnancy and childbirth, only worsened after Lucy Elizabeth's birth. In the midst of his never-ending wartime and personal troubles, Jefferson wished once again to resign. John Page urged him to stick things out. "I know your love of study and retirement must strongly solicit you to leave the hurry, bustle, and nonsense your station daily exposes you to," Page wrote his friend, but "18 months will soon pass away. . . . Deny yourself your darling pleasures for that space of time."

INVASIONS!

At the end of December the American traitor Benedict Arnold led a regiment of loyalists into Virginia. In the early hours of January 4 a servant awaked Jefferson. British ships lay only 25 miles outside Richmond. Arnold's regiment, nearly 1,000 soldiers strong, marched on the capital. Jefferson galloped around the city, directing the evacuation of military supplies. He sent urgent word to Baron von Steuben, the Continental Army commander in Virginia, to speed to Richmond. At one in the morning on January 5, Jefferson joined his family, quickly rushed to Tuckahoe, and moved Martha and the children to another farm farther away. Then he raced to oversee the evacuation of more precious supplies, including 15 tons of gunpowder. His horse collapsed, utterly exhausted. Jefferson yanked off the saddle, grabbed another horse, and continued.

In Richmond, Benedict Arnold sacked Jefferson's house, burned his books and papers, and carried off slaves. The British confiscated what they wanted, including all the tobacco stored in warehouses, set the city aflame, then marched to Portsmouth. The people of Richmond did not know where to find their governor. Arnold had demonstrated how unprepared Virginia was for the worst.

The events armed Jefferson's critics with ammunition—he'd not called up the militias soon enough, he had not taken care of the state's defenses, and he'd shown cowardice by running away. The charges incensed Jefferson. He burned with anger toward Benedict Arnold, offering rewards for the capture of "the greatest of all traitors." Meanwhile, Congress besieged him with requests for food, clothing, and arms. Repeatedly, members of his council failed to show up and take care of business, frustrating Jefferson to no end.

Then, on April 15, sorrow engulfed Martha and Thomas once again when five-month-old Lucy Elizabeth died. With his wife ill and suffering through depression, Thomas had had enough. He did "not wish to leave her" alone, he wrote one council member. Thomas packed up his family and left for Monticello. His term as governor ended June 1 and Jefferson felt ready to resign.

But while the family mourned at Monticello, General Cornwallis unleashed 7,200 redcoats on Virginia in late May 1781. Richmond was again attacked, but with Jefferson at Monticello, he had set up the government temporarily in nearby Charlottesville. George Washington sent the young French general Lafayette to Virginia, but his men numbered less than 1,000, no match for the British. He begged Jefferson to call out more militia to swell his army, but without the assembly, Jefferson told him, "It is not in my power to do anything."

British Colonel Banastre Tarleton struck Charlottesville in hopes of capturing Jefferson. With soldiers nearly on Monticello's doorstep, Jefferson escaped just in the nick of time. While servants hid Monticello's valuables, stuffing the silver under the floor planks, Jefferson hurried Martha, Patsy, and Mary (ages eight and two) into a carriage and sent them to safety. He followed on horseback. The enemy held Monticello for the better part of a day, threatening Martin Hemings, the enslaved butler, but taking only a few bottles of wine when they rode off. Several slaves seized the opportunity to escape.

The British did not spare another of Jefferson's farms. "He destroyed all my growing crops of corn

British Colonel Banastre Tarleton.
COURTESY OF LIBRARY OF CONGRESS

and tobacco," wrote Jefferson. "He burned all my barns" where he stored the harvests from the last year, stole the horses, and fed his army on Jefferson's cattle, sheep, and hogs. Cornwallis's men even burned the fences "so as to leave it an absolute waste."

"CONTEMPLATE THE UNIVERSE"

Jefferson's term as governor ended June 1. Some members of the House of Delegates wanted Jefferson's conduct—his "flight"—investigated. "The inquiry was a shock on which I had not calculated," Jefferson wrote years later. He felt "suspected and suspended in the eyes of the world." The proceedings he confided to James Monroe, his former law student, "inflicted a wound on my spirit which will only be cured by the all-healing grave." In the end the assembly dropped the inquiry, saying it was based on "rumors which were groundless." But Jefferson still seethed at this treatment. A few months later, in October 1781, George Washington, with the aid of French troops and ships, defeated Cornwallis's army at Yorktown, Virginia.

The Jeffersons traveled 90 miles to Poplar Forest, a farm inherited from Martha's father. Jefferson found distraction answering a questionnaire from the French government seeking information about each state. The project suited Jefferson perfectly. He wrote about Virginia's geography, history, farming, the weather, political debates, plants, animals, Native Americans and African Americans, manufacturing, legal cases, and natural history. The writings later became the basis for the only book Jefferson wrote, *Notes on the State of Virginia*.

The spring of 1782 brought visitors to Monticello, Jefferson's friend Lafayette and the Marquis de Chastellux, who left his impressions of Jefferson. At first Chastellux found his host rather cold and serious, but soon felt at ease with an old friend.

> Let me describe to you a man not yet forty, tall and with a mild and pleasing countenance, . . . an American who, without ever having quitted his own country, is at once a musician, skilled

James Monroe, a former Jefferson law student, became Jefferson's friend and political ally.
COURTESY OF LIBRARY OF CONGRESS

> in drawing, a geometrician, an astronomer, a natural philosopher, legislator, and statesman. . . . It seemed as if from his youth he had placed his mind, as he had done his house, on an elevated situation, from which he might contemplate the universe.

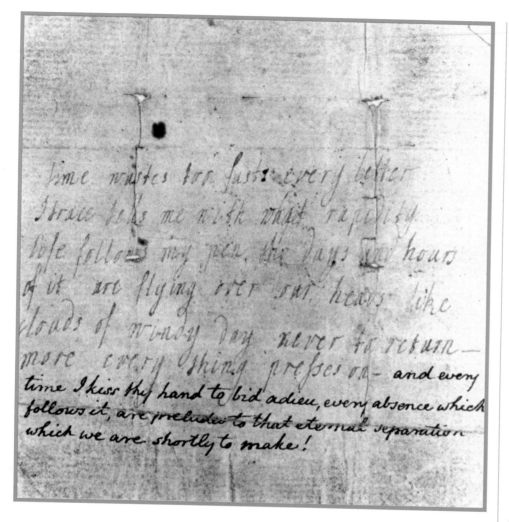

Martha Jefferson's farewell to her husband, finished in Jefferson's hand.

"THAT ETERNAL SEPARATION"

On May 8 Martha gave birth to another baby girl. They named her Lucy Elizabeth after the child who died. Meanwhile, the House of Delegates demanded Jefferson's return. James Monroe urged him to "not decline the service of your country." Worried to the core over his wife's health, Jefferson responded that Virginia had no right to his continual service, he had already "dedicated to them the whole of the active and useful part of my life."

As summer dragged on Jefferson devotedly nursed Martha, taking turns with his sister Martha Carr, his wife's sister Elizabeth Eppes, and Betty Hemings. Patsy later recalled how Jefferson sat beside her mother, "administering her medicines and drink to the last. For four months that she lingered, he was never out of calling. When not at her bedside, he was writing in a small room which opened immediately at the head of her bed."

In early September Martha picked up a pen and began writing from memory lines from *Tristram Shandy*, a book she and Thomas loved and often read to one another. These same words Thomas had written in his commonplace book after Peter died.

> Time wastes too fast: every letter
> I trace tells me with what rapidity
> life follows my pen. The days and hours
> of it are flying over our heads like
> clouds of [a] windy day, never to return—
> more everything presses on

But the effort proved too much. Martha's frail hand failed, all strength gone. Thomas picked up the pen and finished the passage.

—and every time I kiss thy hand to bid adieu, every absence which follows it, are preludes to that eternal separation which we are shortly to make!

Knowing she had little time left, Martha asked Thomas never to marry again. Like other women of the time, she feared a stepmother might neglect or mistreat her daughters.

As Martha slipped into a coma, Thomas nearly collapsed in his anguish. His sister helped lead him from the room. Martha Jefferson passed away September 6, 1782, at the age of 33. Unable to face his empty world, a grieving Thomas barricaded himself in his library for three weeks. He burned all Martha's letters. The quote from *Tristram Shandy* he locked in a secret drawer in his desk wrapped around a lock of Martha's hair.

Thomas finally emerged to spend solitary days walking or riding with nine-year-old Patsy. On their lonely rambles he broke down in grief. "The violence of his emotion to this day I dare not describe to myself," Patsy remembered. "A single event," Thomas wrote, "wiped away all my plans and left me a blank which I had not the spirits to fill up." Where would he go from here, from this darkest void, from this "stupor of mind"?

The Declaration of
INDEPENDENCE.

An American in Paris

In November 1782, a few months after Martha's death, a heartsick Jefferson responded to a letter from Chastellux. His friend's kind words "recalled to my memory that there were persons still living of much value to me." Jefferson knew he must rejoin life. That same month Congress offered Jefferson an escape from grief. They asked him to join the American peace commissioners in Europe. But before Jefferson could sail the following spring, word arrived that a preliminary peace treaty had been signed between the United States and Great Britain. Though Congress no longer needed him, Virginia still did. In June the legislature appointed him a delegate to Congress.

Jefferson's Library

Jefferson owned thousands of books over his lifetime. Periodically he made a catalog of all his volumes. He housed his books in portable pine book boxes that stacked to form bookshelves. Jefferson organized his books by subject, breaking his topics down into three main categories: I. Memory [History and Natural History], II. Reason [Philosophy], and III. Imagination [Fine Arts].

Within those categories he made smaller subsections. History included ancient and modern history as well as natural history, which included sections on physics, agriculture, chemistry and medicine, animals, botany, etc. Philosophy included law, religion, "pure" math, and "physic-mathematical" topics such as optics, astronomy, and geography. The fine arts included gardening, architecture, sculpture and painting, music, and novels, which he listed as epics, romance, tragedy, and comedy.

Part of a letter from Jefferson to his daughter Patsy.
COURTESY OF LIBRARY OF CONGRESS

Jefferson remained busy those few months in 1783 before he left for Congress and a return to public life. He tinkered over a new constitution for Virginia. He returned to a favorite project—revising *Notes on Virginia*. His love of books and his obsession with *buying* books resulted in a library stuffed with 2,640 volumes. Jefferson devoted time to cataloging his immense collection. He also inventoried all his possessions, including his 204 slaves.

Eleven-year-old Patsy accompanied Jefferson to Philadelphia. As Congress moved first to Princeton and then Annapolis, he left his daughter in the care of friends. His letters to Patsy brimmed with schedules for daily lessons and reminders for behaving like a young lady. He meant to prepare Patsy to serve "at the head of a little family of her own," he wrote a friend, confiding his fear that "the chance that in marriage she will draw a blockhead, I calculate at about fourteen to one."

THE NEW NATION BEGINS

Like others, Jefferson harbored fears for the new nation's future. This was the moment to fix things, "while our rulers are honest and ourselves united."

★ ACTIVITY ★ ORGANIZE YOUR LIBRARY LIKE MR. JEFFERSON

Jefferson's library displayed his wide range of interests. Now come up with your own subjects for organizing your family's books, but be sure to include a few of Mr. Jefferson's organizational tips.

WHAT YOU NEED

Notebook

Pen or pencil

Sturdy cardboard boxes set on their side for bookshelves, or use bookcases you already have

Look through your family's books. Do you see groups of subjects? Create a plan like Jefferson's plan to organize your books. Draw a diagram of your library categories in your notebook.

With your family's permission, sort the books into your broadest subjects, grouping similar books together. Now sort again into smaller sub-groups, if needed. Place the books in order into your bookcase.

In your notebook, make a list of all your books under the subject headings. Jefferson also labeled and numbered his books and listed them in his catalog. But unless you have several hundred books (or several thousand like Jefferson), you probably won't need that step.

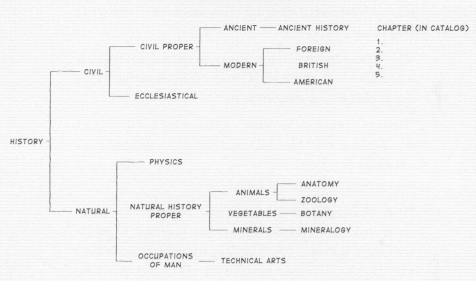

JEFFERSON'S BOOK ORGANIZATION HISTORY EXAMPLE

Fatherly Advice— A Few Samples

In late 1783 Jefferson wrote several letters to Patsy encouraging good behavior and clean clothes. And a little fatherly guilt never hurt either.

- "From 8 to 10, practice music. From 10 to 1, dance one day and draw another. From 1 to 2, draw on the day you dance, and write a letter next day. From 3 to 4, read French. From 4 to 5, exercise yourself in music. From 5 till bedtime, read English, write, etc."

- "I expect you will write to me by every post. Inform me what books you read, what tunes you learn.... Take care that you never spell a word wrong."

- "I have placed my happiness on seeing you good and accomplished, and no distress which this world can now bring on me could equal that of your disappointing my hopes."

- "Never to do nor say a bad thing.... Our maker has given us all, this faithful internal Monitor, and if you will always obey it, you will always be prepared for the end of the world: or for a much more certain event, which is death."

- "Above all things and at all times let your clothes be clean, whole and properly put on. Do not fancy you must wear them till the dirt is visible to the eye.... Nothing is so disgusting in our sex as a want of cleanliness and delicacy in yours. I hope therefore the moment you rise from bed, your first work will be to dress yourself in such a style as that you may be seen by any gentlemen without his being able to discover a pin amiss."

- "Keep my letters and read them at times, that you may always have present in your mind those things which will endear you to me."

"From the conclusion of this war, we shall be going downhill," he lamented. But he knew firsthand how the states had not worked together during the war. Would their squabbles and jealousies and inability to act doom the future? As often happened in times of stress, Jefferson suffered pounding migraines that left him unable to open a book or pick up a pen. Indeed, he could barely even think.

Jefferson believed Congress needed more power. As it stood, Congress had nothing "which would enable them to enforce their decisions," he wrote Edmund Randolph. "The states will go to war with each other in defiance of Congress. One will call in France to her assistance, another Great Britain, and so we shall have all the wars of Europe brought to our doors." The states, felt Jefferson, must give up some power, "placing it in a council of states."

As always, Jefferson worked hard, serving on many committees, penning reports. Still missing his wife, he drove himself mercilessly. But Jefferson felt great frustration with Congress's ability to complete its job. There were seldom enough delegates present to pass anything. Nobody listened to "any logic which was not his own," he complained. The problems started because too many congressmen were lawyers, "whose trade," he noted, "it is to question everything, yield nothing, and talk by the hour." Finally delegates from more states arrived in January 1784 and Congress got down to business, including approving the peace treaty with Great Britain.

In March 1784 Jefferson presented several important proposals to Congress. He submitted a plan to

Jefferson's passport signed by King Louis XVI of France.

COURTESY OF LIBRARY OF CONGRESS

like Metropotamia, Assenispia, Cherronesus, and Pelisipia. Jefferson's plan paved the way for three ordinances passed between 1784 and 1787.

Jefferson proposed slavery be banned in any new states, but Congress rejected this part of his plan by one vote. Jefferson later wrote to a French historian, "The voice of a single individual would have prevented this abominable crime from spreading itself over the new country. Thus we see the fate of millions unborn hanging on the tongue of one man, and Heaven was silent in that awful moment." This marked the last forceful attempt by Thomas Jefferson to oppose slavery.

A NEW APPOINTMENT

In May, Congress appointed Jefferson to join Franklin and Adams in Europe to negotiate trade treaties between the new nation and other countries. Jefferson savored this escape from Congress and

replace the old British coinage system with a decimal system of money based on tens, with a dollar as the basic unit. His Report for a Plan of Government for the Western Territory provided an orderly blueprint for new states to enter the union. He suggested the formation of 10 new states with names rushed back to Monticello to prepare. Patsy would travel with him, but he'd leave little Lucy and Polly behind with Martha's sister Elizabeth.

In early July, Jefferson sailed for Europe along with Patsy, William Short, who'd serve as Jefferson's personal secretary, and James Hemings, a 19-year-old slave from Monticello. "We had a lovely passage in a beautiful new ship," wrote Patsy. "There were six passengers, all of whom Papa knew, and a fine sunshine all the way, the sea as calm as a river." Jefferson made notes during the voyage about the wind, the distances traveled each day, and the sightings of whales and sharks. Once anchored off the French coast they traveled by carriage to Paris, arriving on August 6, 1784.

PARIS!

Jefferson spent part of his first year in Paris seeking a suitable place to live. He hired servants, including a coachman and a Frenchman, Adrien Petit, to run his household. After several moves he finally settled in a home called the Hôtel de Langeac, a three-story villa on the Champs-Elysées. Here he entertained visitors and dignitaries, noblemen, businessmen, artists, and humble American sailors. He filled the stables with a carriage and horses and hired a full-time gardener. He served not only French cuisine but also southern favorites from his garden, such as corn on the cob, sweet potatoes, watermelon, and a Virginia specialty: smoky bacon and hams.

Jefferson indulged his love of shopping and his taste for finery. He rarely passed a bookstore without buying something. He filled the house with furniture and drapes in rich damask fabric. Oriental rugs covered the floors, while engravings, oil paintings, and custom-built bookcases lined the walls. He purchased linens, china, and glassware and rented a piano. Jefferson loved luxury, but he also felt his standard of living necessary to uphold the dignity of America in snooty European eyes. His salary as a foreign minister covered little of this and he sank even more into debt.

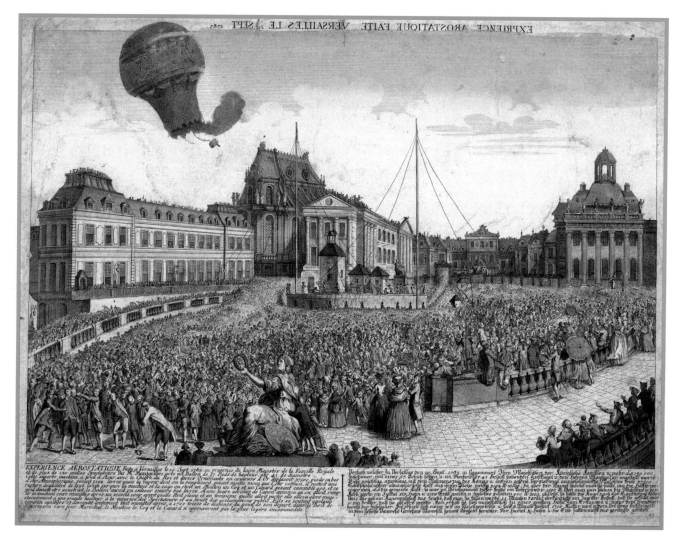

Thousands watch a hot air balloon launch at the Palace of Versailles.

Soon after descending on Paris, Jefferson sent for a tailor and a dressmaker for Patsy. He'd heard that clothes good enough in America would certainly not do in France! Abigail Adams, who'd recently joined her husband in Europe after four years apart, noted "to be out of fashion is more criminal than to be seen in a state of nature [naked]." Along with suits of clothes, Jefferson purchased a new dress sword, shaving brush and razor, silver shoe buckles, and lace ruffles for his sleeves.

61

Those first months he lived like a tourist, strolling amid gardens, riding on horseback through the city, attending concerts, and scouring his guidebook. There were "no words capable of expressing how much I enjoy their architecture, sculpture, painting, music," Jefferson wrote. "It is in these arts they shine."

He also joined thousands of other spectators craning their necks to watch the new craze—the launching of the first hot air balloons, which Jefferson called "the aeronautical art." On one occasion he watched a balloon for over two hours through his telescope.

Sickness struck Jefferson that first autumn as well. "A seasoning, as they call it, is the lot of most strangers," he wrote James Monroe, "and none, I believe, have experienced a more severe one than myself." When his diplomatic duties called, he enrolled Patsy in a Catholic convent school with the daughters of French aristocrats.

JOHN AND ABIGAIL ADAMS

A thoughtful observer and writer, Jefferson skillfully gathered information on European affairs and sent detailed letters to Congress. He worked most closely with John Adams. Though opposites in many ways, the two men became good friends. Where Jefferson disliked confrontation, Adams possessed an aggressive bluntness. The senior diplomat in France, Benjamin Franklin, with his easy ways, often shocked Adams; Jefferson adored Franklin for his wit, wisdom, and scientific work. And while Jefferson felt people could govern themselves by

Benjamin Franklin, whom Jefferson loved and admired.
COURTESY OF LIBRARY OF CONGRESS

following "the dictates of the conscience," Adams felt government must intervene to protect people from their own greed and ambitions. Jefferson agreed with Franklin that the United States owed France a great debt of gratitude for its aid during the war. Adams viewed all things French with suspicion, from the country's Catholic religion to its fashionable, often scandalous society.

Despite their differences, Jefferson admired how John Adams thrust himself into events in a bolder manner than Jefferson ever could. He also admired Adams's intelligent wife and helpmate, Abigail. "Indeed, the man must be a rock," Jefferson wrote her about her husband. "I do not love difficulties. I am fond of quiet, willing to do my duty, but irritable by slander, and apt to be forced by it from my post. These are weaknesses from which reason and your counsels will preserve Mr. Adams."

Over the next two years John and Abigail adopted Jefferson into their family circle. He shared many dinners at their table and enjoyed escorting the Adams children, 19-year-old Nabby and 17-year-old John Quincy, to concerts. Years later, when John Quincy Adams became president of the United States, his proud father wrote Jefferson about "our John." "I call him our John," wrote Adams, because in Paris "he appeared to me to be almost as much your boy as mine."

DIPLOMAT

Clad in his newly tailored clothes and sporting a powdered white wig, Jefferson was formally presented at the French court in October. Together with Franklin and Adams, Jefferson sought trade agreements with European nations, a necessity for the new nation's survival. Europe, however, all but ignored the unlimited trade potential of the fledgling nation, so rich in natural resources.

This tepid interest surprised Jefferson. "They seemed, in fact to know little about us but as rebels, who had been successful in throwing off the yoke of the mother country. They were ignorant of our commerce, which had always been monopolized by England. . . . They were inclined, therefore, to stand aloof." Jefferson also feared Great Britain sabotaged the efforts of American agents. The British press insisted that America stood on the brink of toppling. And Britain still monopolized nearly all of the United States imports.

In the end Jefferson helped negotiate a treaty with Prussia in 1785. He and Adams secured a loan from Dutch bankers to help stem the United States' mounting debt.

The Barbary Coast countries of North Africa—Algeria, Morocco, Tunisia, and Algiers—proved a great headache. They regularly captured American and European ships in the Mediterranean Sea and held the sailors and cargoes hostage. Governments paid these countries huge sums to leave their shipping alone. Jefferson hated paying the tribute, which flicked raw his sense of justice. He wished Congress to refuse payment and send naval ships to show the Barbary Coast countries America could not be bullied and blackmailed. But a navy—which the United States did not possess—would cost more than paying the bribe. The Barbary pirates plagued Jefferson for years, even into his presidency.

NO "FAVORS OF FORTUNE"

In January 1785 Lafayette visited Thomas. He carried letters from Thomas's brother-in-law with the sorrowful news that two-year-old Lucy Jefferson had died. In May, Thomas received a letter from his heartbroken sister-in-law, Elizabeth Eppes, who'd also lost a child.

It is impossible to paint the anguish of my heart.... A most unfortunate hooping cough has deprived you, and us of two sweet Lucys, within a week. Ours was the first that fell a sacrifice.... Your dear angel was confined a week to her bed, her sufferings were great though nothing like a fit. She retained her senses perfectly, called me a few moments before she died, and asked distinctly for water. Dear Polly has had it most violently, though always kept about, and is now quite recovered.... Life is scarcely supportable under such severe afflictions.

He debated if he should send for Polly, but feared the voyage might be too much for her. And could he wrench his small daughter away from her aunt Elizabeth? He wrote an old friend in Williamsburg, "But all the favors of fortune have been embittered by domestic losses. Of six children, I have lost four, and finally their mother."

MINISTER TO FRANCE

In May 1785 word arrived that with Franklin's retirement, Jefferson would become the sole minister to France. Jefferson regarded Franklin as "the greatest man and ornament of the age and country in which he lived." He would miss the old man. And John Adams too was leaving, to become the first American ambassador to Great Britain. The Adamses' departure left Jefferson "in the dumps."

On May 17, 1785, Jefferson joined other diplomats at the glittering Palace of Versailles to meet the king. His footsteps echoed across the marble floors

King Louis XVI of France.
COURTESY OF LIBRARY OF CONGRESS

of the brilliant Hall of Mirrors reflecting candelabras of gold and crystal. Surrounded by aristocrats clad in velvet and lace, Jefferson read a short speech. He doffed his hat at each mention of King Louis XVI or Queen Marie Antoinette. Before leaving the chamber, he bent in three deep bows. At a later meeting Thomas Lee Shippen described Jefferson among the other diplomats at court. "Mr. Jefferson was the plainest man in the room and the most destitute of ribbons, crosses and other insignia of rank [but] he was the most courted and most attended to, even by the courtiers themselves, of the whole diplomatic corps."

But the attention of courtiers was not what he wanted. Jefferson hungered most for news from home. No one wrote to him! "Monroe, I am afraid, is dead," he sarcastically penned a mutual friend. Three boats had arrived from America "without bringing me a line from him or concerning him." He dashed off letters to Elizabeth Eppes pleading for news of Polly. "Pray write to me," he told her, "and write me long letters." To Polly's doctor he wrote, "I can persuade nobody to believe that the small facts which they see passing daily under their eyes are precious to me at this distance." He began plans for Polly to join him in France.

NOTES ON THE STATE OF VIRGINIA

Jefferson returned again to work on his *Notes on the State of Virginia*. As Jefferson wrote Francis Hopkinson, the rest of the world knew so little about America that "we might as well be in the moon." He'd had some copies printed and handed out to a few "particular" Europeans and sent the rest to friends in America. But then he heard a French translation was in the works, a translation Jefferson found "abridged, mutilated . . . a blotch of errors from beginning to end." A London bookseller asked permission to print the English original and Jefferson agreed "to let the world see that it was not really so bad as the French translation had made it appear."

In 1787 *Notes on the State of Virginia* was published with Jefferson's name on the title page.

Jefferson covered a multitude of topics including slavery in Virginia. Jefferson believed African Americans inferior to whites in reason and imagination. He favored a system where blacks gradually became free. But he felt they could not stay in the United States after gaining that freedom. He did not believe the two races could live together in harmony. "Deep rooted prejudices entertained by the whites; ten thousand recollections, by the blacks, of the injuries they have sustained; . . . the real distinctions which nature has made; and many other circumstances, will divide us into parties, and produce convulsions which will probably never end but in the extermination of the one or the other race." If these "convulsions" did come, Jefferson believed, God must favor the slaves suffering in bondage, for "his justice cannot sleep forever."

In addition to educating Europeans about Americans with *Notes on Virginia*, Jefferson also bristled at French arguments that animals, plants, and even people of America were smaller and less developed than those of Europe. Jefferson wanted a moose skeleton and hide dispatched to France to show just how large animals grew in America. He also refuted the charge that America had never produced a great poet, mathematician, or any genius of art or science. America had, claimed Jefferson, produced a Washington and a Franklin! America, he argued was "but a child of yesterday" yet "has already given hopeful proofs of genius." Besides, he reminded Europeans, it had taken many years before

MAKE A SIMPLE MICROSCOPE

Jefferson owned several types of microscopes, magnifiers, and telescopes. In this activity, a drop of water bends light like a lens does to magnify a small object.

WHAT YOU NEED

Empty box of large kitchen matches

Scissors

Transparent tape

Piece of thin transparent plastic (plastic wrap can be used)

Cotton swab

Petroleum jelly

Eyedropper

Water samples from a pond or a small insect to view

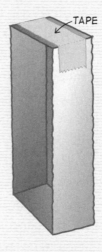

Slide the sleeve off a matchbox. Cut out the center of the matchbook sleeve. Open the closed end of the sleeve, fold down, and tape the side edges.

Cut a piece of plastic to fit the folded end of the matchbox sleeve. Tape the plastic to that end, pulling it tight and placing the tape on the side of the sleeve.

Put a piece of tape on one end of the matchbox tray.

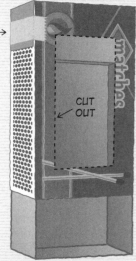

With the plastic-covered end up, slide the matchbox tray into the sleeve with the taped end toward the plastic on the sleeve.

With a cotton swab, smear a circle of petroleum jelly on the plastic. With the dropper, put a single drop of water on the petroleum jelly. Put a drop of pond water or a small insect on the end of the matchbox tray. Slowly slide the sleeve up or down to focus and examine the pond water.

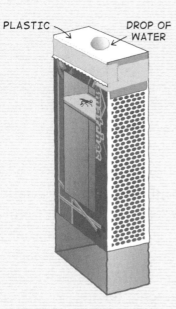

the Greeks "produced a Homer, the Romans a Virgil, the French a Racine and Voltaire, the English a Shakespeare and Milton."

A REBEL IN ENGLAND

In March and April of 1786 Jefferson visited the Adamses in London. Adams was negotiating a new treaty that would open the British West Indies to American trade and finally remove Great Britain from forts in the American West. America also demanded payment for slaves and other property taken by Britain during the war. But British merchants owed money from before the war wanted their payment, too, and they wanted it in gold or silver, not worthless American money.

Like many Americans, Jefferson suffered financial losses during the war that made it hard to pay off his debts. He'd sold land to raise money, only, "I did not receive the money till it was not worth oak leaves," he told one of his creditors. He had little sympathy as the British stalled and ignored the American diplomats. "With this country," Jefferson advised Congress, "nothing is done. . . . The nation is against any change of measures." To the American envoy in Spain, William Carmichael, Jefferson wrote, "I consider the British our natural enemies and as the only nation on earth who wish us ill from the bottom of their soul." If Jefferson had his way, Americans would lessen their ties with British trade and instead enjoy free trade with the rest of the world.

On March 17, 1786, Adams presented Jefferson to King George III. The king walked about a large circle, speaking to each person, who then bowed away from his majesty's presence. No one knows exactly what happened that day, but years later both Jefferson and the Adams family recalled the king's rude behavior to the two Americans. It seemed the king had not forgiven the long list of crimes Jefferson accused him of in the Declaration of Independence. When Jefferson and Adams bowed to the king and queen, they looked up to see the royal backsides—their majesties had turned their backs on the once rebellious duo, a deliberate snub in front of the whole diplomatic corps! Recalling the incident in his autobiography, Jefferson labeled George III narrow-minded and mulish.

As frustrating as diplomacy proved, Jefferson enjoyed sightseeing with Adams, and he especially admired English gardens. He loved the natural feel of sweeping lawns, wandering paths, canals, wilderness areas, clumps of trees, and shrubs. He toured William Shakespeare's home, the Tower of London, and the British Museum, and attended six plays. He visited a mill run by a new invention, the steam-powered engine, and sat solemnly while American artist Mather Brown painted his portrait.

Jefferson also shopped like a man with no worry about debt. He bought a copying press for his writing and ordered a harpsichord for Patsy. He ordered a new carriage and leather goods, such as horse saddles and bridles, trunks, and boots. And then there were the scientific instruments! Jefferson purchased an expensive telescope, a protractor, a thermometer, a theodolite, and a microscope.

Back in Paris, Jefferson accepted a challenge from friends in Virginia: plan and design a new

An important feature of ancient Greek and Roman buildings, columns have been used by architects ever since. Jefferson used all three "orders" of column capitals—the top decorative part of the column—in his architecture. He used Doric capitals at Monticello and Poplar Forest. His buildings at the University of Virginia have examples of each.

ADULT SUPERVISION REQUIRED

WHAT YOU NEED

Cardboard paper towel tube

4-inch square of Styrofoam, 1 inch thick

Pencil

Craft knife or sharp kitchen knife

Ruler

2 dowel rods, 36 inches by $\frac{1}{8}$ inch

Glue

Tape

Bakeable sculpting clay (like Sculpey)

Old newspapers

Spray paint (white, silver, bronze, gold)

Hold a tube on the center of a Styrofoam square and firmly trace around it with a pencil, making a trench. Use the craft knife or a sharp kitchen knife to cut out a square around the hole. Then punch it out.

Mark around the tube 1 inch from the top and the bottom. Mark and cut the dowel rods into four 9-inch pieces using the craft knife.

Glue the dowel rods around the tube, spaced $\frac{1}{2}$ inch apart. Set them between the 1-inch border

DORIC

CORINTHIAN

IONIC

line drawn at the top and the bottom. Tape the dowels at the top and the bottom with small pieces of tape. This holds the dowel in place while the glue sets.

For the Ionic and Doric columns, press the clay flat and decorate. You will need a capital for the back and front.

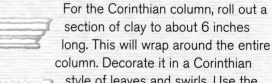

For the Corinthian column, roll out a section of clay to about 6 inches long. This will wrap around the entire column. Decorate it in a Corinthian style of leaves and swirls. Use the craft knife to slice a clean edge. Bake the capitals according to package directions, usually at 275° Fahrenheit for 15 minutes for every ¼ inch of thickness. Let cool when done.

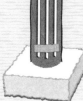

Glue your capital to the top of the column. Let dry.

On a layer of old newspaper, spray the column with white, silver, bronze, or gold paint. Set the column down into the Styrofoam base.

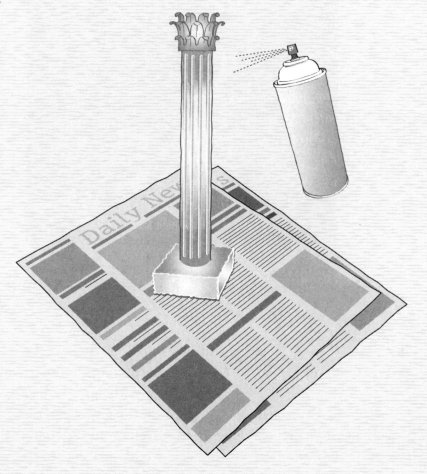

the approbation of nearly 2,000 years." To cap off his design he commissioned famed sculptor Jean-Antoine Houdon to create a statue of George Washington for the building.

MARIA COSWAY

In August 1786 the painter John Trumbull introduced Jefferson to artists Richard Cosway and his wife, Maria. Rumors flew that Richard treated his wife cruelly and unfaithfully. Maria, like her husband, painted miniature portraits. A lovely woman with brilliant blue eyes and blonde curls, Maria sang, played music, and entertained with grace—she instantly captivated Jefferson. For the next few months he spent every moment he could with her, basking in Maria's company, "every moment . . . filled with something agreeable."

In mid-September Jefferson fell, shattering his wrists with the right bone protruding through the skin. Maria visited him over the next few weeks as Jefferson dealt with his painful injury, made more painful by the news that she must return to London. When Maria left, Jefferson wrote her a long letter "seated by my fireside, solitary and sad." He created a dialog between his head and his heart over the misery of missing her.

> *Head.* Well, friend, you seem to be in a pretty trim.
>
> *Heart.* I am indeed the most wretched of all earthly beings. Overwhelmed by grief . . .
>
> *Head.* . . . This is one of the scrapes into which you are ever leading us.

Portrait of Jefferson by Mather Brown, 1786.
NATIONAL PORTRAIT GALLERY, SMITHSONIAN INSTITUTION; BEQUEST OF CHARLES FRANCIS ADAMS

Capitol Building for Richmond. Awed by the revival of Greek and Roman architecture transforming Europe, Jefferson decided Richmond needed a Greek temple. Out with the English Georgian style of architecture! Jefferson designed the building, then had a plaster model made and shipped to Virginia. His plans were "copied from the most precious, the most perfect model of ancient architecture remaining on earth, one which has received

Jefferson fell for artist Maria Cosway while in France.
LIBRARY OF CONGRESS

Heart. Oh my friend! This is no moment to upbraid my foibles. I am rent into fragments by the force of my grief! If you have any balm, pour it into my wounds. . . .

Head. The art of life is the art of avoiding pain.

Jefferson told Maria she must write him often and "say many kind things . . . they will be food for my soul." The two had planned a trip to Italy, the land of Maria's birth. Now he decided he would go alone. From March through June 1787 Thomas Jefferson hit the road.

THE TRAVELER

Jefferson hoped his travels would spur new trade ties with Italy. He planned a route through southern France then into Turin and Milan in Italy. Keeping his identity secret, he traveled in a small carriage with a hired driver and planned to hire what servants he needed along the way. Jefferson gawked at "curiosities" in each town and rambled through fields and farms, examining the crops, the soil, and the lives of the people. He attended the theater and

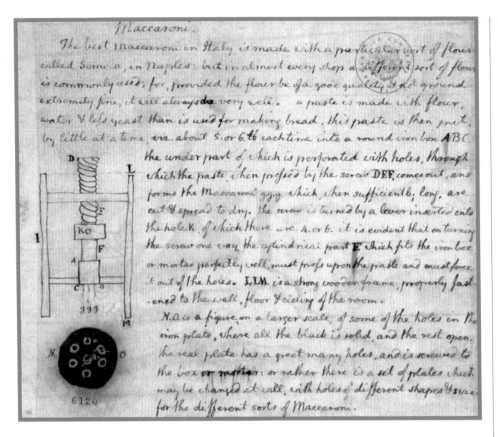

Jefferson's drawing of a pasta-making machine.
COURTESY OF LIBRARY OF CONGRESS

visited healing waters for his ailing wrists. Jefferson passed through fishing villages studying trade in port cities. He traveled over the Alps by mule, loving the bracing clean air.

He observed women toiling in the fields alongside men, an indication to Jefferson of extreme poverty. "Men in a civilized country never expose their wives and children to labor . . . as long as their own labor can protect them from it." He blamed the peasants' suffering on the nobility. It never occurred to him that slave women at Monticello also labored in the fields.

And then there was the food, glorious food—Jefferson loved fine dining. He soaked up lessons on winemaking, visited vineyards, and ordered cases of wine. He discovered groves of olive trees—could this be a new cash crop for America? He took cuttings to send back to America. He secretly gathered, and smuggled out, Italian rice as another possible new crop for America. He studied raisins, new varieties of figs, capers, almonds, and pistachio nuts in hopes that all could be grown in the American South. He saw how Parmesan and mascarpone cheeses were made, toured dairies, and studied icehouses that stored the cheese. He even learned how to make ice cream.

He reveled in Roman ruins—baths, arches, roads, and temples. "I am immersed in antiquities from morning to night," he wrote a friend. He loved the air, the light, the golden glow of the countryside. "I am in the land of corn, vine, oil, and sunshine," he wrote William Short. "What more can a man ask of heaven?"

For the return journey Jefferson traveled mostly by boat, the quickest means available, and arrived in Paris on June 10, 1787. He wrote Maria, "Why were you not with me? So many enchanting scenes which only wanted your pencil [to draw]. . . . When are you coming here? If not at all, what did you ever come for? Only to make people miserable at losing you."

Maria did visit again and stayed four months with a friend. But Jefferson did not see her as often as before. Diplomatic affairs kept him busy. Time

BAKE A MACARONI [AND CHEESE] PIE

Jefferson became interested in making macaroni (his term for all types of pasta) while in Italy. He even purchased a pasta-making machine. Jefferson did not invent macaroni and cheese, but he probably helped make pasta popular in the United States by serving it during his presidency. One dinner guest, who was not impressed, referred to the dish as "a pie called macaroni." A recipe for making macaroni, written by Jefferson, still survives today.

ADULT SUPERVISION REQUIRED

WHAT YOU NEED

8 cups water

4-quart pan

1 tablespoon salt

2 cups uncooked elbow macaroni

Large colander

2 cups half-and-half

Glass measuring cup

3-quart pan

2 tablespoons butter

2 tablespoons flour

Whisk

¼ teaspoon Tabasco sauce

½ teaspoon kosher salt

Pinch of pepper

Large spoon

½ cup shredded Swiss cheese

1½ cups shredded sharp cheddar cheese

9-inch-by-10-inch pie pan

½ cup shredded sharp cheddar for topping

Broccoli florets (optional)

In the larger pan bring about 8 cups of water to a boil. Add 1 table-spoon of salt. Pour macaroni into the boiling water and cook following package directions. Place the colander in the sink; when the pasta is cooked, empty the pan into the colander and let the pasta drain.

Warm the half-and-half in a glass measuring cup or bowl in the microwave. In the other pan melt the butter. When the butter is melted add the flour. Over medium heat mix and whisk for about a minute.

Add the half-and-half and whisk until everything is mixed. Slowly stir until the sauce begins to bubble and thicken. This will take several minutes. Add the Tabasco, kosher salt, and pepper. Then remove the sauce from the heat—this is important so the cheese melts smoothly.

Using a spoon, stir in the Swiss cheese until it melts into the sauce. Next, stir in the cheddar cheese until it melts into the sauce. Your sauce should be thick and smooth.

Add the cooked and drained macaroni to the sauce. Stir carefully, folding the macaroni into the sauce. Mix well and pour into a pie pan. Sprinkle with the remaining cheese.

Bake in a preheated 350°F oven for 30 minutes.

Optional: Add 1 cup of broccoli florets to the recipe. Cook the broccoli the last few minutes with the pasta and drain with the pasta.

and space pulled them apart as longer silences spread between letters. Eventually those heady days with Maria Cosway became a memory Jefferson treasured, but he moved on.

POLLY

In July 1787 nine-year-old Polly finally arrived in Paris. Three years had passed since Lucy died and Jefferson first thought of bringing Polly to France. "I am sorry you have sent for me," she wrote him. "I don't want to go to France. I want to stay with Aunt Eppes." For Polly, her father was a stranger.

Polly's traveling companion on the long voyage was her enslaved maid, 14-year-old Sally Hemings, sister of James Hemings. The girls landed first in England and stayed with John and Abigail Adams, who ordered them new clothes. Abigail praised Polly's charm and intelligence but had a warning for Jefferson, too. "I show her your picture," Abigail wrote, but "she says she cannot know it, how should she when she should not know you."

When Jefferson pleaded he had too much work to personally bring his daughter to Paris, Abigail wrote her disapproval. The girl had "depended upon your coming for her. She told me this morning that as she had left all her friends in Virginia to come over the ocean to see you, she did think you would have taken the pains to have come here for her, and not have sent a man whom she cannot understand. I express her own words."

Soon after Polly arrived in Paris, Jefferson placed her in the same school with Patsy and saw his daughters on weekends.

Abigail Adams, wife of John Adams, a woman Jefferson greatly admired.
COURTESY OF LIBRARY OF CONGRESS

THE CONSTITUTION

Back in the United States, delegates gathered to strengthen the Articles of Confederation decided instead to scrap that document and start over with a new plan for the American government. From May through September 1787, members battled, argued, compromised, and in the end produced the Constitution of the United States. Benjamin Franklin was the oldest member of the convention and George Washington presided over the meetings. Jefferson's dear friend James Madison helped lead the new constitutional movement. As the states debated the document and prepared to vote for or against it, Madison sent a hot-off-the-presses copy to Jefferson in November 1787.

A little toughening up of the Articles of Confederation, like granting Congress power to regulate trade, would have satisfied Jefferson. He believed people overreacted to Shays's Rebellion, a single instance of resistance "honorably conducted." To William Smith he noted, "God forbid that we should ever be 20 years without such a rebellion. What signify a few lives lost? The tree of liberty must be refreshed from time to time with the blood of patriots and tyrants."

He especially worried about the role of the president. Everyone knew George Washington would be elected the first president of the United States, a man admired and trusted. But what would happen when Washington stepped down? Would the presidency slide into monarchy? "I was much an enemy to monarchy before I came to Europe," he wrote Washington. "I am ten thousand times more so since I have seen what they are ... there is not a crowned head in Europe whose talents or merits would entitle him to be elected vestryman by the people of any parish in America."

But as the battle over ratification raged in America, Jefferson declared himself neutral. All he urged, as did many, was that a bill of rights, "what the people are entitled to against every government on earth," be added to the Constitution.

This "beautiful example of a government reformed by reason alone without bloodshed" pleased him greatly. To Madison he wrote, "The example of changing a constitution by assembling the wise men of the state instead of assembling armies will be worth as much to the world as the former example [the American Revolution] we had given them."

In March and April 1788, Jefferson left Paris again. He worked with Adams in Holland to negotiate further loans from the Dutch, followed by a trip through the Rhine country of Germany. He continued efforts to pry open more French markets to American trade. One small victory allowed the sale of more American tobacco. Jefferson also watched with interest and worry the growing tensions in French politics.

"AWAKENED BY OUR REVOLUTION"

Troubles bombarded France: the country faced heavy debts, many people had no jobs, taxes burdened the middle class, droughts plagued French farmers, and the price of bread—the main food of the poor—skyrocketed. Mobs roamed Paris erupting into riots. "Paris is now become a furnace of politics," noted Jefferson.

Desperately needing money, King Louis XVI in May 1789 gathered together the Estates General for the first time in 150 years. Three groups made up the Estates General: the nobles, the church, and the Third Estate, the taxpaying citizens. Jefferson believed "a revolution" in the French Constitution seemed inevitable. He hoped for peaceful change

REVEIL DU TIERS ETAT.

A political cartoon shows aristocrats and clergy reacting with horror as the Third Estate awakens, throws off their chains, and reaches for a gun. The Bastille looms in the background.

COURTESY OF LIBRARY OF CONGRESS

and reform but feared that the poor and uneducated people he'd seen on his travels "are not yet ripe for receiving the blessing to which they are entitled." France, he wrote Madison, "has been awakened by our revolution. They feel their strength, they are enlightened."

On May 5, 1789, Jefferson attended the opening of the Estates General at Versailles. The event gathered the diplomatic corps, the royal court, and 1,200 delegates. The king and queen sat on their thrones, enrobed in silks and velvets, jewels, gold, and silver. The ministers of state attended in all their splendor of ribbons, sashes, and medals. Three hundred priests sat in their robes of scarlet, black, and white. On long rows of benches sat the representatives of the people.

But the Estates General deadlocked on how to vote. The Third Estate decided to meet without the nobility and clergy and declared themselves a National Assembly on June 17. Jefferson believed "the king is honest and wishes the good of his people" but the idea of shaking up the "hereditary aristocracy is too difficult a question for him."

Violence invaded politics. On July 12, rioters burned the Customs House, a symbol of the hated taxes. Jefferson watched armed groups "roaming all night through all parts of the city." The next day Lafayette organized a citizen's militia to restore order, but the militia broke into shops grabbing red, white, and blue ribbons and made cockades for their hats. On July 14, Jefferson sat with friends when he heard that angry mobs had stormed the Bastille, a royal prison.

Lafayette and like-minded reformers met secretly at Jefferson's house. Together they drafted a charter of rights for the French people and discussed a new French Constitution. Jefferson believed constitutions needed regular change and revising, explaining to Madison, "No society can make a perpetual constitution or even a perpetual law. . . . The earth belongs to the living and not to the dead."

The document hammered out at Jefferson's home served as the model for the French Declaration of the Rights of Man, which Lafayette presented to the National Assembly. The assembly "mowed down a whole legion of abuses," Jefferson wrote John Jay in August, abolishing all titles of rank and all the privileges.

Jefferson had asked Congress for a leave of absence to return to Virginia. He had business at home, and after hearing 16-year-old Patsy speak of becoming a nun, Jefferson hoped to introduce her to a few eligible American suitors. Congress, however, had its hands full setting up the new government and ignored his request for months. But in September 1789 Jefferson prepared to return to America.

His five years in Europe had been happy, filled with architecture and paintings, lovely gardens, rich foods and wine, polished society, and fascinating friendships that satisfied his artistic soul. As he wrote Maria Cosway before his ship sailed, "We have left a turbulent scene, and I wish it may be tranquilized on my return, which I count will be in the month of April. . . . Remember me and love me." But Jefferson did not return to France or ever see Maria again. When he arrived back in Virginia in late November, he learned that a new job awaited him.

LE GÉNÉRAL LA FAYETTE

The Marquis de Lafayette fought in the American Revolution as a young man, then helped usher in new freedoms in his native France.
COURTESY OF LIBRARY OF CONGRESS

"The Hated Occupations of Politics"

When his ship anchored at Norfolk, Virginia, Jefferson learned President Washington offered him the post of secretary of state. Unsure what he really wanted, Jefferson postponed his decision. In Richmond he toured the new Capitol Building he'd designed and received warm wishes from the Virginia Assembly. Richmond must have seemed small and plain compared to the grand boulevards vibrant with thousands of people, the imposing architecture, and the lush gardens of Europe.

A month after landing at Norfolk, Jefferson and the girls reached Monticello. Many of the plantation slaves mobbed the carriage, unhitched the horses, and pulled the family up the road to the house. Years later Patsy described the slaves' reaction: "Such a scene I never witnessed in my life.

Jefferson arrives home at Monticello after his years in Europe.
LIBRARY OF CONGRESS

When the door of the carriage was opened, they received him in their arms and bore him to the house, crowding round and kissing his hands and feet, some blubbering and crying, others laughing." Indeed, for the enslaved people of Monticello Jefferson's return marked an end to the rule of overseers for Jefferson's more evenhanded control.

After a whirlwind courtship of two months, 17-year-old Patsy wed her third cousin, Thomas Mann Randolph, at Monticello in February 1790. As a wedding gift Jefferson presented the couple with 1,000 acres of land and 25 slaves. Patsy, most often called Martha now, settled on an estate only a few miles from her old home.

SECRETARY OF STATE

After several months pondering his future, Jefferson finally accepted Washington's offer to join the new government. Somehow, politics always reeled him back. Jefferson realized he wanted a hand in shaping American affairs.

On March 1 he left Monticello for the three-week journey to New York City, the seat of the federal government. Jefferson rented a house far below his standards in Paris, but he added a library in hopes of improving it. He missed his daughters, writing Martha, after "having had yourself and dear Poll to live with me so long. . . . I feel heavily the separation from you."

The State Department consisted of himself, two clerks, two assistant clerks, and a translator. Jefferson earned a $3,500 yearly salary and oversaw a department budget of $8,000. Besides Jefferson, Washington's cabinet included the secretary of the treasury, Alexander Hamilton; the secretary of war, Henry Knox; and Jefferson's cousin Edmund Randolph as attorney general. The cabinet wrote reports and brought policy ideas to Washington for debate and approval. John Adams served as vice president.

Before Jefferson took office, Alexander Hamilton's Report on the Public Credit proposed the federal government take over the unpaid war debts of the states. But many southern states opposed this plan— they had already paid off much of their debt. Why should they pay taxes to support a state like Massachusetts, which was still mired in debt? Jefferson feared a failure to compromise would "burst and vanish" the nation's credit "and the states separate to take care everyone of itself." Both the new nation's standing in the world and American trade would suffer.

Jefferson agreed to nudge southerners to pass Hamilton's bill. But in return he required the permanent capital of the country be moved south to a site on the Potomac River. Jefferson hoped to undermine the influence of merchants and bankers in the middle and northern states. Instead, let the new Federal City lie in the rural south, free from the corruption of a large city.

THE BANK BILL

Hamilton next proposed that the government create a national bank and boost American manufacturing. He hoped to raise American credit and power with the rest of the world and also ease the money shortage at home. Growth of American manufacturing would set the new nation on more equal terms with Europe and make the United States less dependent on buying everything overseas.

Hamilton's proposals awakened Jefferson's sense of unease. The two men viewed America's future in far different terms. Soon Jefferson regretted helping Hamilton pass the debt bill, claiming Hamilton had made him "a tool for forwarding his schemes not then sufficiently understood by me."

In February 1791 Jefferson sent Washington his opinions on Hamilton's plan to establish a

The Capitol Building in Richmond designed by Thomas Jefferson.
COURTESY OF LIBRARY OF CONGRESS

national bank. For Jefferson, and a growing number of men around him, this plan pressed too far—the Constitution did not grant Congress power to set up a national bank. Jefferson argued for a strict construction, or reading, of the Constitution. Congress could not "do anything they please." To take a single step beyond the Constitution's boundaries "is to take possession of a boundless field of power."

Hamilton believed his programs delivered the strength and security the new nation desperately needed. The secretary of the treasury felt the Constitution *implied* that the government had authority to create the bank as part of its power to

81

Alexander Hamilton

Alexander Hamilton was born with nothing, an illegitimate son abandoned by his father and orphaned by the death of his mother. He rose from poverty to attend King's College [now Columbia] and in 1777 became an aide-de-camp to General Washington, eventually earning a field command. After the war Hamilton qualified for the New York bar. He worked tirelessly for the new national constitution. During the ratification battle in the states Hamilton, along with James Madison and John Jay, penned a collection of essays called *The Federalist*, which helped win approval of the Constitution. Brilliant, quick-thinking, and determined, Hamilton proved a ready foe for Thomas Jefferson.

Alexander Hamilton, secretary of the treasury and Jefferson's political foe.
COURTESY OF LIBRARY OF CONGRESS

regulate trade. There must be some leeway, argued Hamilton, or the Constitution would never meet the needs of changing times.

Jefferson's fears went beyond questions over the Constitution, however. The bank bill, along with Hamilton's plan to encourage manufacturing, laid bare a path for a few men to grasp great amounts of wealth and power. The government would only partly control the bank. The bank would also have private investors. This seemed a shortcut to the abuses and corruption he'd despised in the aristocratic courts of Europe.

For Jefferson, Hamilton's plans trampled every republican value he'd hoped for America after the revolution. In Jefferson's perfect vision, America remained a nation of small farmers, sensible and good people, who required less—not more—government interference and control. And while

Hamilton favored continued trade ties with Great Britain, Jefferson wished to slash American trade with the British in favor of increased trade with France and the rest of the world.

Washington considered the opinions of Hamilton, Jefferson, and Attorney General Randolph, but in the end the president sided with Hamilton's views on the Constitution and his plan for strengthening America. Little by little Jefferson's distrust of

Hamilton shifted onto Washington, too; he doubted the president's dedication to the ideals of the revolution. In the Senate, Jefferson's ally James Madison led the losing battle against the bank bill.

As Jefferson and Hamilton's disagreements over domestic policy, the economy, and foreign affairs festered into a personal and bitter feud, Washington, who admired both men, stood caught in the middle.

Jefferson as secretary of state, around 1791, by artist Charles Willson Peale.

INDEPENDENCE NATIONAL HISTORICAL PARK

Republicans and Federalists

Supporters of Thomas Jefferson called themselves Republicans. They believed a strong central government threatened citizens' liberties. There should be as little government control as possible over people's lives. Instead, power should rest with the people in each state. "The People" meant white, property-holding male voters. But citizens had responsibilities—Jeffersonian Republicans felt that only an educated population could handle self-government. Republicans envisioned a nation of small farmers not dependent upon Federalist strengths like trade and business. In foreign affairs, Republicans favored France. They believed the French Revolution was inspired by America's own quest for freedom and liberty—the "spirit of 1776," as Jefferson often called it.

At the time of the United States' founding, a Federalist was someone who supported adopting the Constitution. The word came to mean those who supported the idea of a strong federal government. Federalists feared too much power resting with the people led to mob rule. They did not trust the common man. People needed a strong government based on the rule of law to keep order, peace, and happiness. In foreign affairs, Federalists admired Britain's system of trade and centuries-old laws. Like Hamilton, Federalists supported an American economy that bolstered trade, small factories, and banking. The New England states became a stronghold for Federalist politicians.

"THE TREASURY AGAINST THE PEOPLE"

When the government moved to Philadelphia in November 1790, Jefferson remodeled a large house to fit his needs and surrounded himself with treasures arrived from his mansion in Paris—books, wine, a fountain, furniture, paintings, and even boxes of pasta. He built a large carriage house for his three carriages and five horses. His maître d'hôtel, Adrien Petit, arrived along with James Hemings to prepare the French cuisine Jefferson loved. Thirteen-year-old Polly shared the house with her father.

But even as Jefferson settled into his comfortable and aristocratic nest, he harbored misgivings over Washington's formal weekly gatherings and the way the president drove about the city on official occasions in a coach pulled by six horses. It all appeared a bit too kingly for Jefferson's taste.

In spring 1791 Jefferson penned a preface for Thomas Paine's new book *The Rights of Man*. "Something is at length to be publicly said against the political heresies which have sprung up among us," wrote Jefferson. "I have no doubt our citizens will rally a second time round the standard of *Common Sense*." Jefferson's barb at the "heresies" against true republicanism aimed squarely at the Federalists. Readers up and down the coast knew it. The bitter squabbles that inflamed Washington's cabinet behind closed doors were no longer secret. Two political factions emerged: Jefferson and his "Republican" followers against Hamilton and the Federalists.

Jefferson and Madison hired Philip Freneau to start a newspaper to compete with the pro-Federalist papers. Freneau's paper, the *National Gazette*, debuted at the end of October 1791. Jefferson also hired Freneau as a translator and paid the editor with State Department money. He allowed Freneau access to "all my letters of foreign intelligence." Jefferson and Madison sold subscriptions to keep the presses churning. In return for this support Jefferson asked Freneau to "give free place to pieces written against the aristocratical and monarchical principles."

Jefferson instructed Madison and others to sharpen their quills on Hamilton's reputation. The *National Gazette* warned readers, "It is the Treasury of the United States against the people.... The influence which the treasury has on our government is truly alarming; it already forms a center, around which our political system is beginning to revolve." Meanwhile, Hamilton summed Jefferson up as a man "of political mysteries and deception ... he circulates his poison thro' the medium of the *National Gazette*."

WASHINGTON SEEKS PEACE

The war of words spewing from the nation's newspapers distressed Washington greatly. His two secretaries flung charges "that stand in need of evidence for their support," said the president. Washington eventually wrote Jefferson and Hamilton asking both men for cooperation and reconciliation. How regrettable it was, Washington wrote Jefferson, that with enemies all around, it was the internal fights "tearing our vitals." The president urged Jefferson to have "more charity for the opinions and acts of" others. Wasn't there a line "by which both of you could walk"? "I do not see," wrote a saddened Washington, "how the Reins of Government are to be managed, or how the union of the United States can be much longer preserved.... Melancholy thought!"

Jefferson accepted no blame for the government's rift. Hamilton's behavior, he wrote Washington, "flowed from principles adverse to liberty, & was

George Washington hated the war of words between Hamilton and Jefferson.

COURTESY OF LIBRARY OF CONGRESS

his paper, they certainly concern me not," he told Washington. Jefferson denied using his influence with members of the legislature "to defeat the plans of the Secretary of the Treasury." But Jefferson *had* used his influence, even attempting in early 1792 to instigate an investigation into Hamilton's conduct of treasury business.

Hamilton admitted his part in the newspaper wars but claimed he did so only to protect his reputation. Out of respect and affection for Washington he promised "to smooth the path of your administration and to render it prosperous and happy."

But the battle lines were drawn. Jefferson and Hamilton loathed each other. Each saw only a dangerous enemy who sought to drive him from office. Each man viewed the other's plan for America with horror—there was no room for compromise. In the fall elections of 1792, Jefferson's followers worked hard to elect Republicans and gain control of Congress.

"A LITTLE INNOCENT BLOOD"

In April 1793 news reached America that the French government had beheaded King Louis XVI and declared a new French Republic. France and Great Britain were at war, and Prussia, Spain, and the Netherlands were soon dragged into the conflict. To protect the new nation as it struggled to gain strength, Washington declared America neutral in the wars engulfing Europe. The Republican press blasted Washington, charging his neutrality actually favored Great Britain and hurt France. Jefferson noted that the press attacked the president due

calculated to undermine and demolish the republic." When asked about his role, Jefferson falsely claimed he had no idea Freneau would criticize the government. "As to the merits or demerits of

Washington receives "citizen" Genet, minister from the French Republic.

COURTESY OF LIBRARY OF CONGRESS

to "the love of the people to France and its cause, which is universal."

Jefferson felt the chaos and bloodshed of the French Revolution would eventually sweep freedom across Europe. Even when French friends were arrested or beheaded beneath the guillotine's blade, Jefferson supported the French Revolution. He hoped for victories by the army of the French Republic over the gathering forces of the monarchies of old Europe. "The liberty of the whole earth," Jefferson wrote William Short, became the prize for "a little innocent blood." "We surely cannot deny any nation the right whereon our own government is founded," he penned, "that every one may govern itself under whatever form it pleases, and change the forms at its will." For Jefferson, failure in France could spell failure in the United States, a "falling back to that kind of half-way house, the English Constitution."

Washington agreed to Jefferson's request that he receive the new minister sent by the French Republic, Edmund Genet. Heartened by Jefferson's warm responses, Genet incited problems from the moment he arrived in Philadelphia in May 1793. He meddled in American affairs and jeopardized Washington's declaration of neutrality. Genet recruited American sailors and ships for privateer missions against Britain. He attempted to raise men to march against Spanish territories in the Southwest and had a French ship drag a captured British vessel into Philadelphia. He also encouraged "Democratic-Republican" societies that met across America in support of France. Jefferson warned Genet to stop, but by August the cabinet demanded Genet be recalled back to France. Hamilton wanted Jefferson's letters to Genet made public, hoping to embarrass the Republicans, but Washington refused this.

RETIREMENT

On August 11, 1793, Jefferson wrote Washington that he wanted to retire. He was disgusted, often driven to bed by migraines and stressed by "the circle which I know to bear me peculiar hatred, that is to say the wealthy aristocrats, the merchants connected closely with England, the new created paper fortunes." Washington wanted to quit, too. But Jefferson and others urged the president to stay for a second term, pleading the country would fracture without him. "North and South will hang together," wrote Jefferson, "if they have you to hang onto." Washington reluctantly agreed. Jefferson officially resigned as secretary of state, effective December 31, 1793.

He spent the next three years in retirement, barely venturing more than seven miles from home. "I am eating the peaches, grapes, and figs of my own garden," he wrote Maria Cosway in 1795. "I am become . . . a real farmer, measuring fields, following my ploughs, helping the haymakers. How better this than to shut up in the four walls of an office, the sun ever excluded." In fact, Jefferson determined to never again rejoin "the hated occupations of politics and to remain in the bosom of my family, my farms, and my books."

The farms included nearly 11,000 acres divided into seven separate holdings. But much of the land remained forest instead of cultivated fields producing crops. Jefferson began a seven-step plan of crop rotation to save his soil, which had been depleted from years of growing tobacco. He planted corn, wheat, and over a thousand fruit trees. He fired new

A portrait of Jefferson copied from an 1805 Gilbert Stuart painting.
COURTESY OF LIBRARY OF CONGRESS

red-clay bricks, mended fences, watched over the brewing of cider, and hoped to turn his grape harvest into wine.

Deeply in debt, Jefferson tried to make his farms more efficient and sought other means of making money. A nailery set up on Mulberry Row—the lane at Monticello where skilled slave craftsmen

In an attempt to make Monticello more self-sufficient, Jefferson set up a spinning and weaving shop. Here a handful of Monticello's enslaved young women worked with spinning wheels and looms. Jefferson expected the women to weave at least 1,200 yards of cloth a year. Try your hand at a simple method of weaving.

WHAT YOU NEED

Scotch tape

Yarn (you can use two colors or a multicolored skein)

8-inch-by-12-inch Styrofoam board or bread board (you can use a larger surface, too)

Ruler

Scissors

Tape one end of the yarn to the back of a board (long side) and wind the yarn around the board, about 8 to 12 threads per inch. When the board is wrapped, cut off the excess yarn and tape the loose end in place. These are the *warp* threads.

Cut several 3-foot lengths of yarn. Wrap one end of one piece with tape. This will make it easier to weave in and out.

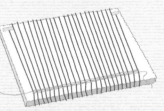

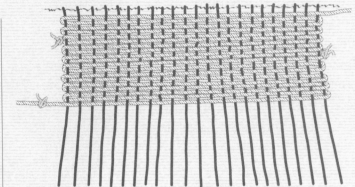

Weave the new yarn in the opposite direction than you wrapped the board. This is called the *weft*. Let part of your yarn hang off the board and start weaving the yarn over and under the warp. When you reach the end, start back in the other direction.

Tighten the weave as you go by pushing the threads together with your fingers.

To begin a new piece of yarn, tie it onto the old piece (after you've taken the tape off) and keep weaving with a new taped end.

To finish, cut the warp threads on the back and tie them off into knots. Start at one end, tie the first two warp threads together, then move on all the way around the woven cloth. Trim the long ends.

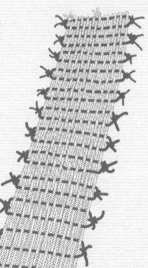

worked and lived—became his most profitable venture. Enslaved boys ages 10 to 16, such as Wormley Hughes, Burwell Colbert, and Joe Fossett, worked long, hot hours hammering and cutting nails, closely supervised by Jefferson. Jefferson rode his farms in the morning and spent the other half of the day "counting and measuring nails," he wrote John Adams. In 1796 the boys delivered a ton of nails each month. "From [ages] 10 to 16," wrote Jefferson, "the boys make nails, the girls spin. At 16 [they] go into the ground [the fields] or learn trades."

Jefferson designed a more efficient moldboard for his plow. The design won him a gold medal from the Société d'Agriculture in Paris in 1805. He also built a smaller, horse-powered threshing machine to harvest wheat more quickly. And establishing a sawmill meant plenty of wood on hand for his biggest project, his greatest labor of love: renovating and expanding Monticello.

MONTICELLO

Jefferson ignored the tremendous cost and plunged into a total rebuilding project. He reported to George Wythe that he was "living in a brick-kiln" as he prepared to demolish the old eight-room house. By 1796 Monticello's unfinished state forced Jefferson to warn a potential guest, "The noise, confusion, and discomfort of the scene will require all your . . . patience." Amid heaps of lumber and bricks and wood skeletons for rooms, Jefferson oversaw his ode to the classical architecture he'd loved in Europe. Over the next 13 years or so he doubled the size of

Joe Fossett

Betty Hemings's grandson, Joe Fossett, born in 1780, spent his childhood making nails, running errands, and working in the main house. Jefferson picked 16-year-old Joe, a quick, bright, and skilled lad, to train as a blacksmith. Eventually Joe Fossett ran the blacksmith shop at Monticello, where he shod horses; made, sharpened, and repaired farm tools; forged carriage parts; and as one man remembered, "could do anything it was necessary to do with steel or iron." Fossett also did blacksmithing work for neighboring farmers on the side—Jefferson let Joe pocket a portion of the money he earned.

Jefferson freed his talented blacksmith in his will, but he did not free Fossett's wife or children. This forced Joe Fossett to bargain with several white men in the neighborhood so they would buy his family and then let him purchase their freedom as he earned the money. In the 1830s Joe, his wife Edy, a former Monticello head cook, and some of their children left Virginia for a new home in Ohio.

his house, creating three floors with 21 rooms topped by a rotunda, the first on any American home.

The main floor would house 11 rooms, including the Hall, which came to serve as display space for a wealth of maps, Native American objects, mammoth bones, and curiosities. The family gathered in the parlor for games, reading, and music beneath walls laden with 48 works of art. The Jeffersons enjoyed meals in a formal dining room and a small, informal tearoom. Jefferson's apartment took up one side of the house for his book room, his cabinet (or study), his two-storied bedroom, and a small greenhouse. Each of his rooms flowed into the next. The top floors boasted nine bedrooms, while storage cellars

Many of Thomas Jefferson's floor plans and architectural drawings survive today. Try your hand at designing your dream bedroom suite—or an entire house or building—drawn as if you were looking down into it. This is called a floor plan. *Next, draw the outside of the house or building, as if you are looking straight ahead at it. This is called an* elevation *or a* facade.

WHAT YOU NEED

Graph paper

Ruler

Pencil with eraser

Watercolors and brush (optional)

Architecture books for inspiration—historic and modern houses (or just design a futuristic building from your imagination)

If you're planning on drawing multiple rooms, every square on the graph paper can equal one foot of wall length. For a single room, each inch of squares can equal a foot, or whatever size scale you'd like. Measure the size of your room and draw the walls with the ruler and pencil, using the graph lines to keep things straight. Your room does not have to be a square—include interesting nooks and crannies.

Show where doors will go by erasing the wall line and making an arc, like the path of a door that has swung open. If you are making a floor plan with multiple rooms, be sure your doors open somewhere without striking anything.

Show windows by using a double shaded-in line.

Show other features of the room: a fireplace, a closet, built-in shelves, even furniture placement.

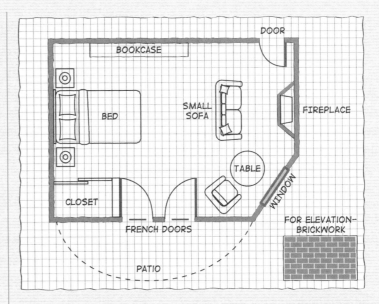

Use a new sheet of graph paper for each floor of your building. Be sure the floors match up!

Using a sheet of graph paper, draw the front elevation of your building or room. Show all the floors, doors, windows, architectural elements such as columns, domes, stairs, and chimneys, and the roofline. Draw a section with brick or siding to let the viewer know what the building is made of.

If you want, use a wet brush to lightly wash the drawings with watercolor paints.

For his bedroom Jefferson designed an alcove bed, a skylight in the roof, and a closet with portholes above the bed for storage.
MONTICELLO/PHOTOGRAPH BY ROBERT LAUTMAN

Monticello's Entrance Hall housed a buffalo robe, mammoth bones, maps, and other artifacts.
MONTICELLO/PHOTOGRAPH BY CHARLES SHOFFNER

filled the lowest level. Jefferson designed or selected everything for Monticello, from the draperies to the wood moldings to the china.

Two long L-shaped terraces, one on either side of the house, provided space where the family strolled or sat outdoors. Unseen beneath the terraces, slaves worked in the *dependencies*, including the kitchen, smokehouse, laundry house, icehouse, dairy, carriage house, and several slave living quarters.

Jefferson's style of living included as little contact with his slaves as possible. A moving cart, or dumbwaiter, laden with food allowed Jefferson and his guests to dine with few servant interruptions. An overseer recalled that "there were no Negro and other [outbuildings] around the mansion, as you generally see on plantations." The slaves he dealt with most often face-to-face were the light-skinned Hemings family, many of them related to his wife.

Of all the enslaved people at Monticello, more is known about Betty's youngest son, John Hemings, than any other. A master carpenter and joiner, Hemings left behind letters and his beautiful creations in wood—cabinets, chairs, mantel pieces, and carved arches. Born in April 1776, John began his career as a field-worker and an "out-carpenter" building fences, barns, and granaries.

When Jefferson began remodeling Monticello in the 1790s, John Hemings trained alongside the skilled white joiners and carpenters Jefferson hired. Hemings worked as the main assistant, finishing all the decorative woodwork in Monticello before stepping into the top job himself. Jefferson knew he had a talented craftsman; he paid Hemings an annual tip of $20.

Hemings not only built furniture and created impressive moldings and railings. He also built plows, looms for weaving, and worked on Poplar Forest. Jefferson's grandchildren called Hemings "Daddy" and referred to John often in their letters. In 1826 John Hemings received his freedom in Jefferson's will. A widower, he died suddenly in 1833.

A French visitor noted that "Mr. Jefferson's slaves, who, neither in point of colour or features, showed the least trace of their original descent; but their mothers being slaves, they retain, of consequence, the same condition."

"THE SECOND OFFICE"

Burying himself away on his mountaintop affected Jefferson. "My health is entirely broken down," he wrote Madison in 1795. Seven years later he recalled those days in a letter to Polly, who, like Martha, married a distant cousin, John Wayles Eppes, in 1798.

I am convinced our own happiness requires that we should continue to mix with the world, and to keep pace with it as it goes; and that every person who retires from free communication with it is severely punished afterwards by the state of mind into which they get. . . . I can speak from experience on this subject. From 1793 to 1797, I remained closely at home, saw none but those who came there, and at length became very sensible of the ill effect it had upon my own mind, and of its . . . tendency to render me unfit for society, and uneasy . . . it will be a lesson I never shall forget as to myself.

Slowly Jefferson rejoined society. He began caring again, aroused by several political events. In the fall of 1794 George Washington led a force of 1,500 soldiers against an uprising of farmers infuriated by a new tax on whisky. Turning their corn into whisky proved the cheapest and most profitable way to get their crop to market. For Jefferson, the use of an army to enforce a federal tax law—a Hamilton tax!—smacked of tyranny. He directed Madison to keep him informed but to do it "behind the curtain."

When news of a new treaty with Great Britain, known as the Jay Treaty, exploded on the political scene, Jefferson condemned it as an "infamous act." For Republicans the treaty proved too pro-British, even at America's expense. The document, they claimed, ended any so-called American neutrality.

Jefferson showcased Native American objects in Monticello's Entrance Hall, including a large Mandan buffalo robe painted with a battle scene. Native Americans of the plains depended on buffalo for food, clothing, shelter, household objects, and utensils. Some hides, like Jefferson's, featured painted decorative symbols or told a story in pictures.

WHAT YOU NEED

Brown paper grocery bag
Scissors
Spray bottle with water
Paints and brush
Crayons or colored markers
Pencil

Cut a paper bag open so it lies flat, then cut off the rectangle that was the bottom of the bag.

Cut out the shape for your buffalo robe.

Lightly spray the "hide" with water, then crunch up the bag in your hands. Unfold it carefully and scrunch it up again. Repeat a few times until the hide wrinkles and softens, looking old and weathered. Small tears are OK, or they can be taped shut on the backside.

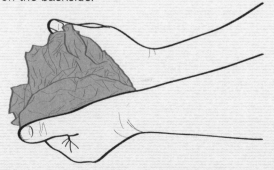

Draw your story design, or decorate the robe with symbols using animals, plants, geometric shapes, mountains, rivers, etc.

Paint or color the robe and hang it on a wall or door. To make a larger robe, tape several paper bags together—after you have scrunched them but before you cut out the shape.

PAINT A COMPASS ROSE

Jefferson had an octagonal compass rose painted on the ceiling of Monticello's Northeast Portico. He connected it to a weathervane on the portico's roof. Jefferson could stand inside the house, look up at the compass rose, and see which direction the wind blew. Jefferson's compass rose had a black background with greenish-blue for the directions and center "rose."

ADULT SUPERVISION REQUIRED

WHAT YOU NEED

Scissors or utility knife

Large square of poster board or cardboard

Old newspapers

Can of spray paint

Paints and brush

Ruler, yardstick, or tape measure

Pencil

Navigational compass (optional)

Poster-mounting gum

Using the scissors, cut the four corners off a square sheet of poster board to make an octagon.

Outdoors, lay the octagon on newspapers and spray paint it whatever color you wish. Let dry.

In each corner of the octagon paint a direction initial in this order: N (North), NE (Northeast), E (East), SE (Southeast), S (South), SW (Southwest), W (West), NW (Northwest). Let dry.

Measure across the center of the octagon. Divide the number of inches in half and mark the spot with your pencil. Do the same thing across the other direction. Now you have the center of your compass rose.

Paint a design in the center of your compass that reaches toward the directions.

Hang the compass rose for decoration on your bedroom ceiling. Which direction does your room face? Use a navigational compass or observe where the sun rises (toward the east) or sets (toward the west). Place the compass rose so that the directions face the right way. Then, with adult permission, stick the compass rose on the ceiling with the mounting gum.

With Washington stepping aside after two terms as president, the scramble began for the nation's highest office. Friends implored Jefferson to stand against the main Federalist candidate, John Adams. Jefferson had felt that what "little spice of ambition which I had in my younger days has long since evaporated." But he could never fully deny the lure of politics.

Madison wrote Monroe, "the republicans knowing that Jefferson alone can be started with hope of success mean to push him." By spring of 1796, with his consent or not, Jefferson was running for president. Knowing Jefferson remained cool to the idea, Madison confided to Monroe, "I have not seen Jefferson and have thought it best to present him no opportunity of protesting . . . against being embarked on this contest."

Would "the Republican Jefferson or the Royalist Adams" be president, demanded Republican handbills. Federalists attacked Jefferson for fleeing his post while Virginia governor during the war, for quitting as secretary of state, and for leading a pro-French party aiming to overthrow the government.

In five states people voted to choose electors, and those electors then voted for president. In most states members of the assemblies selected the electors. When all the electors' votes were counted, Adams nudged out Jefferson for the presidency, 71 electoral votes to Jefferson's 68. As the second-place finisher, Jefferson became vice president. He surprised his friends by accepting the "second office," which Jefferson said "is honorable and easy. The first is but a splendid misery. If Mr. Adams can be

John Adams, second president of the United States.
COURTESY OF LIBRARY OF CONGRESS

induced to administer the government in its true principles and relinquish his bias to the English constitution," Jefferson would willingly stand by his old friend. "He is perhaps the only sure barrier against Hamilton's getting in," he added.

On March 2, 1797, Jefferson returned to Philadelphia. A banner strung over the street greeted him: "Jefferson the Friend of the People." He was sworn in as president of the senate, the main official

The American Philosophical Society

Benjamin Franklin founded the American Philosophical Society in 1743 to promote the study of "useful knowledge" in a wide spectrum of arts and sciences. Franklin wished "all . . . experiments to let light into the nature of things." In 1797 the American Philosophical Society chose Thomas Jefferson as its president, an honor he deeply enjoyed. "I feel no qualification for this distinguished post," Jefferson wrote, "but a sincere zeal for all the objects of our institution, and an ardent desire to see knowledge so disseminated [spread] through the mass of mankind." To acknowledge Jefferson's work in natural history, the society named a two-leafed plant after Jefferson, the *Jeffersonia diphylla*.

The two-leafed Jeffersonia diphylla.

job of the vice president. The first task he undertook was writing *A Manual of Parliamentary Practice*, a guide for how the senate conducted business, published in 1801. In 1826 the House adapted Jefferson's manual for its use, too. Much of Jefferson's parliamentary handbook is still used today.

Feelings of goodwill and cooperation between Adams and Jefferson quickly fizzled. While still in retirement in 1796, Jefferson had written a letter to his friend Philip Mazzei, who lived in Italy, furiously attacking government officials, merchants who traded with England, bankers, and all Federalists, including Adams and Washington, for wanting to turn America into a new Great Britain filled with aristocrats. "It would give you a fever," wrote Jefferson, were he to name the leaders of the American Revolution, "men who were Samsons in the field and Solomons in the council," who now bowed down to corrupt England. European papers reprinted Jefferson's letter, and a year later his words recrossed the Atlantic to America, in May 1797. In the backlash that followed, Washington stopped writing to Jefferson. Adams, too, felt stabbed in the back. To prevent another such embarrassment, Jefferson asked friends *not* to let his letters out of their hands.

THE XYZ AFFAIR

The war in Europe continued eroding politics in America. Adams chafed that France treated the United States "neither as allies or friends nor as a sovereign state." Tensions between the two nations escalated since the Jay Treaty. France had seized nearly 300 American merchant ships heading to British ports in North America, the Caribbean, and the Mediterranean. In this charged atmosphere, Adams dispatched three commissioners to negotiate outstanding disputes with the French government.

French agents, known only as X, Y, and Z, told the three American negotiators in Paris that peace talks would continue only if the Americans agreed to pay huge bribes and John Adams formally apologized for comments he'd made about France. The American envoys, Charles Cotesworth Pinckney, John Marshall, and Elbridge Gerry, refused.

Adams reported events to Congress in March. Fearing a looming war with France, he urged Congress to protect American shipping by building a navy and voting for money to defend American shores. Republicans in Congress thought Adams *wanted* a war, and Jefferson labeled the president's policies toward France "insane." They pressed Adams to hand over the XYZ papers, believing the president concealed the truth. But the papers showed the bribery and arrogance of the French and engulfed the country in a wave of anti-French feelings, embarrassing the Republicans.

"THE REIGN OF WITCHES"

That summer of 1798 Congress voted further steps to defend and protect the government, including the Alien and Sedition Acts. The Alien Act allowed the president to imprison or deport any foreigner he considered "dangerous to the peace and safety" of the United States, especially during wartime. The Sedition Act made it illegal for Americans to

The Sedition Act

During the 18 months that the Sedition Act was in effect, the government tried 14 cases against writers, editors, and publishers, convicting and imprisoning 10 men. Jefferson offered money to help support some of these men, including James Callender, sentenced to nine months in jail for attacking Adams in his anti-Federalist book *The Prospect Before Us*. Callender sent Jefferson proof sheets for the book and received encouragement from the vice president. Jefferson hoped such writings would "inform the thinking part of the nation [and] set the people to rights." In the end, however, Jefferson's trust in Callender proved misplaced. Within a few years, Callender turned his pen against his former supporter.

oppose the government through "any insurrection, riot, unlawful assembly" or to write, speak, or publish "any false, scandalous, and malicious writing." Federalists feared that words had the strength to erode loyalty and topple both the government and the nation.

Jefferson considered the Sedition Act a violation of the Constitution's first amendment—the federal government had no power to pass such a law! For Jefferson, the Sedition Act served only one purpose: to silence Republican newspapers. Jefferson feared even sending his letters through the mail in case federal officials monitored his writings. At the end of June he wrote John Tyler, "A little patience and we shall see the reign of witches pass over, their spells dissolved, and the people recovering their true sight, restoring their government to its true principles."

But Jefferson did not sit patiently. By October he and James Madison had drafted resolutions to block the Sedition Act at the state level. Jefferson's resolutions were introduced into the Kentucky legislature, Madison's into Virginia's legislature. The states, penned Jefferson, had not joined together to give "unlimited submission to their general government." Instead, they had granted only "certain definite powers" to the national government. When the national government "assumes undelegated powers, its acts are . . . void and of no force."

In November 1798 the Kentucky legislature adopted Jefferson's resolutions, declaring the Sedition Act null and void. Jefferson's Kentucky Resolutions, written while he was still vice president, blackened his reputation even more in Federalists' eyes.

"AS REAL A REVOLUTION"

In 1796 Jefferson had drifted along with supporters who wanted him to stand for president. But throughout 1799 he prepared to lead his Republican forces into battle. The time had come, he wrote Madison, for "energies and sacrifices. The engine is the press. Every man must lay his purse and his pen under contribution." Jefferson proclaimed his confidence "in the good sense of the American people" to protect freedom and liberty.

He escaped to Monticello, devoting himself to his home and farms for months. But he also crystallized his thoughts for the upcoming elections. He called for peace "even with Great Britain," and disbanding the army in times of peace to save money. He called for free trade between all nations. The Constitution

must be kept "according to the true sense in which it was adopted by the States," keeping for the states every power they did not specifically turn over to the government or the president. Jefferson longed for "a government rigorously frugal and simple, applying all the possible savings of the public revenue to the discharge of the national debt."

Still, Jefferson stayed behind the scenes as much as possible, warning supporters, "Do not let my name be connected with the business." He relied on trusted allies like Madison and Monroe, Republican newspapers, and pamphlets to spread his political message.

The presidential campaign of 1800 featured gossip, ridicule, and scandal. The Federalists had splintered between those supporting Adams and those loyal to Hamilton. Hamilton urged his followers to abandon Adams after the two men bitterly argued over Federalist cabinet members turning to Hamilton for advice. Now Republicans trumpeted their message: Federalists equaled monarchy and corruption. The president's son, diplomat John Quincy Adams, dressed and sauntered like a young prince, and the most hated Federalist, Alexander Hamilton, had an affair with another man's wife.

Federalists attacked Jefferson's religious views, his luxurious and expensive tastes, and his pro-French connections (did Americans want guillotines set up in town squares?), and whispered that he'd long ago chased after his best friend's wife, an embarrassment Jefferson acknowledged. Yale University president Timothy Dwight proclaimed Jefferson's election meant the destruction of churches and "the

Jefferson's draft of the Kentucky Resolutions.

COURTESY OF LIBRARY OF CONGRESS

Bible cast into a bonfire." New York Republican Aaron Burr, a great foe of Hamilton, and Federalist Charles Pinckney also stood for their parties.

On December 3, 1800, electors met in their states and voted for the next president. By the end of the month everyone knew the results—the vote tied, 73–73, between Jefferson and Burr. Adams finished third with 65 votes, a deep humiliation to the president. Now, the House of Representatives would decide the outcome.

House members determined to keep voting, even sleeping and eating in the unfinished Capitol building, until they named a winner. Jefferson's supporters expected Burr to declare himself unworthy of the office and throw his votes to Jefferson, but the proud New Yorker refused. Voting began on February 11, 1801, with no decision until February 17, when on the 36th vote several Federalists threw in blank ballots as did one Burr supporter, giving Jefferson the election. Aaron Burr became vice president. The Federalist Party never regained its former power.

In small part, Jefferson owed a nod to Hamilton, who despised Burr even more than he did Jefferson. Since December, Hamilton had written to fellow Federalists, "There is no doubt that, upon every virtuous and prudent calculation, Jefferson is to be preferred. He is by far not so dangerous a man and he has pretentions to character. As to Burr, there is nothing in his favor. His private character is not defended by his most partial friends."

Aaron Burr.
COURTESY OF LIBRARY OF CONGRESS

For Jefferson, his election equaled a new and bloodless revolution, "as real a revolution in the principles of our government as that of 1776 . . . not effected indeed by the sword . . . but by the rational and peaceful instrument of reform, the suffrage of the people."

"By Which I Most Wish to Be Remembered"

Boasting little more than muddy roads still blemished with tree stumps and some half-done buildings, Washington, D.C., celebrated its first taste of a presidential inauguration on March 4, 1801. Jefferson, a month away from his 58th birthday, left his boardinghouse and walked the short distance to the Capitol building. An escort of congressmen and Virginia militia officers kept step alongside the new president. A newspaper reported Jefferson's clothes were "as usual, that of a plain citizen without any distinctive badge of office." Indeed, for the great occasion Jefferson did not don an elegant suit or wear a ceremonial sword. The men gathered in the Senate Chamber, the only finished room inside the Capitol.

The President's House around 1810.
COURTESY OF LIBRARY OF CONGRESS

In his speech that day Jefferson spoke of peace with the Federalists. "Every difference of opinion is not a difference of principle," he said, speaking softly as usual so that spectators strained to hear him. "We have called by different names brethren [brothers] of the same principle. We are all republicans: we are all federalists."

Jefferson pledged justice to all men "of whatever state or persuasion, religious or political." He called for "peace, commerce, and honest friendship with all nations, entangling alliances with none." He promised "a wise and frugal government, which

shall restrain men from injuring one another, which shall leave them free to regulate their pursuits of industry and improvement, and shall not take from the mouth of labor the bread it has earned. This is the sum of good government."

Chief Justice of the United States John Marshall, a leading Federalist with an agile, brilliant legal mind and a fellow Virginian, administered Jefferson's oath of office. An underlying tension marked both men. A new Judiciary Act had gone into effect February 13 allowing President Adams to appoint 16 federal judges and name a new chief justice to the Supreme Court. Adams finished his appointments on March 2, igniting irate Republicans over the last-minute "midnight appointments" that handed Federalists control of the court system. Jefferson called Adams's action "indecent conduct in crowding nominations after he knew they were not for him." The friendship of Thomas Jefferson and John Adams smashed upon the rocks of politics—they would not write or speak to each other for over a decade.

MR. PRESIDENT

Jefferson might have offered soothing words in his inaugural speech, but within days he penned Monroe he would not befriend the Federalists "whom I abandon as incurable and will never turn an inch out of my way to reconcile." Jefferson stripped many Federalists of their jobs and replaced them with Republican supporters. He assembled a cabinet of trusted friends and like-minded men, such as James Madison as secretary of state. But just to play it safe, Jefferson seldom held a full cabinet

Jefferson tried to walk or ride horseback daily for exercise.

meeting. "The method of separate consultations prevents disagreeable collisions," he noted.

Jefferson rose at five o'clock in the morning and organized his day, tackling paperwork until nine. As always he preferred to work alone, secluded with his thoughts and his writings. Jefferson wrote all his own letters and drafted many of the bills he wanted passed. At nine o'clock he met with cabinet members or important visitors before a return to his paperwork. Jefferson required daily exercise to stay healthy and sharp; he nearly always slipped from behind his desk for a long horseback ride in the afternoon. Most often people found Jefferson "dressed, or rather undressed, with an old brown coat, red waistcoat, old corduroy small clothes, much soiled, woolen hose, and slippers without heels," recalled Senator William Plumer of New Hampshire.

Three times a week the president sat down at 3:30 P.M. to a lengthy dinner that included a dozen or more invited guests. For these occasions he dressed elegantly in black suits with silk stockings, crisp white shirts, and his hair powdered. The meals featured the French food and wine (sometimes eight different kinds) that Jefferson adored. His wine bill alone for his first term ran nearly $10,000. The president paid for the dinners out of his $25,000 a year salary and typically, by the end of the year, he'd slid about $4,000 more into debt. Jefferson seldom held formal diplomatic events or receptions—perhaps he'd suffered through enough of those in Europe! Martha sometimes traveled to Washington and served as her father's hostess at the President's House.

Two enslaved young women brought from Monticello, Fanny Gillette and Edith Fossett, trained under Jefferson's French chef. For most of the next eight years, the women had their children with them, but their husbands remained at Monticello. Fanny and "Edy" prepared many presidential feasts and earned a two-dollar tip each month. Guests often mentioned the delicious food, especially a luscious dessert with an ice cream ball wrapped "in covers of warm pastry."

After dinner, Jefferson often worked late into the night, scribbling letters, reading, thinking, sitting 10 to 13 hours a day at his writing table. For three weeks in the spring and the months of August and September, when Congress adjourned, Jefferson escaped to Monticello. He relaxed into managing his farms and enjoying life among his growing brood of grandchildren.

"MONTICELLAN SALLY"

In September 1802 James Callender, the editor Jefferson championed during the Sedition Act, turned against Jefferson for refusing him a government post. Callender published the first rumors that Thomas Jefferson fathered children with Sally Hemings, one of his slaves. Federalist papers splashed the story across the country, providing lurid details of Jefferson's trysts with "Black Sal," the "African Venus." Jefferson never responded to the accusations. He left no clue at all about his relationship with Sally Hemings, but his family denied the charge for years.

Many slave owners took advantage of enslaved women and fathered children with them. By law, any child born to an enslaved woman was also enslaved. "I consider a woman who brings a child every two years as more profitable than the best man of the farm," Jefferson wrote in 1820.

Born a slave in 1773, Sally Hemings may have been the half sister of Thomas Jefferson's wife, Martha. Another slave later described Sally as "mighty near white . . . very handsome, long straight hair down her back." Jefferson's grandson Thomas Jefferson Randolph described Sally as "light colored and decidedly good looking."

Sally belonged to Jefferson since she'd been a toddler. She sailed to France with Polly and trained as a lady's maid, learning to care for the clothing and needs of Patsy and Polly Jefferson. According to Hemings family tradition, the relationship between Sally and Jefferson began in France. Sally agreed to return to Virginia from France, where she'd be freed from slavery, if Jefferson promised to free her children.

At Monticello Sally's duties included "such light work as sewing," according to her son Madison. Sally's first child was born in 1795, a daughter who died in 1797. Over the next 14 years Sally Hemings bore Thomas Jefferson five more children: William Beverly was born in 1798, another daughter was born and died in 1799, daughter Harriet was born in 1801, son James Madison was born in 1805, and another boy, Thomas Eston, was born in 1809. The boys were called by their middle names. Jefferson listed the birth of Sally's children in his Farm Book just as he recorded the births of other slaves.

Though Sally's children grew up in bondage, they did not remain so. Harriet and her brother Beverly vanished from Monticello around their 21st birthdays. Their brother Madison later revealed they lived as white people, shedding any trace of their enslaved ancestry. Jefferson freed Eston and Madison in his will. He did not free Sally, but she walked away from her mountaintop home after Jefferson's death and lived with her sons in Charlottesville.

MR. JEFFERSON AND THE COURTS

After the Sally Hemings scandal, Jefferson feared that some newspapers did go too far. He avoided any taint of Adams's Sedition Act, though. Instead, Jefferson quietly encouraged state officials to prosecute Federalist editors in local courts for the crime of seditious libel.

Jefferson signed Congress's repeal of the Adams Judiciary Act of 1801. But he still had those pesky Federalist judges to deal with. Some of the commissions for new judges appointed by John Adams had not been delivered before Adams left office. Jefferson ignored the commissions. One of the Federalist appointees, William Marbury, petitioned the Supreme Court to force the government to deliver his commission in a case known as *Marbury v. Madison*.

Chief Justice John Marshall ruled that Marbury had a right to his commission and lectured Jefferson for not fulfilling this duty. But Marshall also asked whether the court had the power to force the government to deliver the commission. And here he argued that the original Judiciary Act of 1789, which

Chief Justice John Marshall.
COURTESY OF LIBRARY OF CONGRESS

granted the court this power, differed from the Constitution. So Marshall decided the court must go with the Constitution over an act of Congress. He denied Marbury's petition and decreed the Judiciary Act of 1789 unconstitutional. In his February 1803 decision, Marshall affirmed the court's powers to interpret the Constitution and to wield judicial review—the power to decide whether a law is constitutional and strike down unconstitutional laws.

Jefferson won the case, but Marshall enhanced the Supreme Court's power. For Jefferson, judicial review granted too much power to a handful of judges. But Marshall had outfoxed him. "When conversing with Marshall," exclaimed Jefferson, "I never admit anything." With his clever "twistifications," Marshall could force you "to grant his conclusion. Why if he were to ask me if it were daylight or not, I'd reply, 'Sir, I don't know, I can't tell.'"

Jefferson encouraged Republican congressmen to impeach troublesome Federalist judges. In May 1803, after reading a scathing decision from Supreme Court Judge Samuel Chase, Jefferson urged that Chase's "attack on the principles of our Constitution" not go unpunished. But as always, Jefferson preferred to work behind the scenes. One elderly judge was impeached and removed, but Chase survived his impeachment trial in the Senate.

A FOREIGN AFFAIRS GIFT

Jefferson's first years in office were busy ones. As promised, he pushed Congress to economize, slashing military spending and lopping off "useless offices." Jefferson hoped that "a just and friendly conduct on our part will procure justice and friendship from others." But he was not against using American military power when needed.

One of his first tests arrived in May 1801 when the Pasha of Tripoli declared war on the United States over tribute money. Jefferson ordered a naval squadron to North Africa to protect American shipping. The small-scale naval war against the Barbary pirates dragged on throughout most of his presidency. Stephen Decatur's 1804 rescue of American sailors held hostage in the Bay of Tripoli thrilled the nation.

Napoleon Bonaparte.
COURTESY OF LIBRARY OF CONGRESS

The Napoleonic Wars sweeping Europe proved Jefferson's most thorny foreign problem. Jefferson wanted free trade with both France and England. But he worried about France's expanding empire planted on America's back doorstep in the lands west of the Mississippi River. Over one million Americans lived in the West, and "the Mississippi

106

[River] is to them everything," Jefferson wrote. Secretly he sent Monroe to France as a special envoy. Would Napoleon sell some of this land to the United States? Jefferson was willing to spend up to $9 million on the deal.

Yet before Monroe reached Paris, the French government summoned envoy Robert Livingston to a meeting in April 1803. Napoleon needed money for his wars in Europe. He had no desire to defend French territory in America from the British up in Canada. And he'd just had a French force wiped out on the Caribbean island of Santo Domingo during a slave revolt led by Toussaint-Louverture. Napoleon wanted out of North America. He would sell the entire Louisiana Territory including the Mississippi River, around 800,000 acres in all, to the United States for $15 million.

A stunned Livingston quickly agreed. By the end of April Livingston and Monroe signed documents that nearly doubled the size of the United States. Jefferson's great triumph also worried him—was the deal even constitutional? But he abandoned an attempt to draft a constitutional amendment—there just wasn't time. The House and Senate ratified the treaty for purchasing the Louisiana Territory in October 1803, with no questions about its constitutionality—this deal was too good to pass up! In December France officially handed over the new lands.

EXPLORATION WEST

Even before Napoleon offered this great bargain to the United States, Jefferson planned to send a small expedition to explore up the Missouri River and beyond to the Pacific Ocean. Ever curious about nature, Jefferson never stopped recording the weather, the flights of migrating birds, his study of plants, and the bones of animals. During his many years away from home, he asked family and friends to observe and report back. To Polly he wrote, "I hope you have, and will continue to note every appearance, animal and vegetable, which indicates the approach of spring, and will communicate them to me."

In Washington he sometimes escaped work to roam the riverbanks, woods, and hills. A female friend noted, "Not a plant from the lowliest weed to the loftiest tree escaped his notice." The president waded into swamps, clambered over rocks "to obtain any plant he discovered or desired, and seldom returned from these excursions without a variety of specimens."

On June 20, 1803, Jefferson penned a long list of instructions for his secretary, Captain Meriwether Lewis, the man he'd named to lead the expedition along with Lieutenant William Clark. During their journey, wrote the president, the team should map the land, rivers, and natural landmarks and record the weather. They must take note of "the soil and face of the country, its growth and vegetable productions, especially those not of the United States, the animals of the country generally, and especially those not of the United States; the remains and accounts of any which [may] be deemed rare or extinct . . . the dates at which particular plants put forth or lose their flower or leaf, times of appearance

A passionate weather tracker, Jefferson purchased many instruments like thermometers and barometers, including traveling varieties, to help him. He also recruited friends and family to supply him with weather reports from other places.

WHAT YOU NEED

Access to a television, newspapers, or a computer
A journal
Pen or pencil

Use modern tools to keep a weather journal. Turn to daily newspapers, television weather forecasts, and the Internet for up-to-date information to record in your journal. You can also paste photographs of weather events into your notebook.

Use friends or family who live in different regions to help you, or take a sample of weather in different cities around the nation on the computer. Compare notes on what is happening.

Here are your instructions, straight from Thomas Jefferson, as written to his friend James Madison: "I wish you would keep a diary under the following heads or columns." Draw 12 columns onto your weather journal page. Label them and fill them as Jefferson describes below.

- First column: day of the month

- Second and third columns: the temperature and barometric pressure at sunrise

- Fourth and fifth columns: temperature and barometric pressure at 4 P.M.

- Sixth and seventh columns: the wind direction at sunrise and 4 P.M.

- Eighth and ninth columns: weather conditions of rain, snow, fair, windy, etc., at sunrise and 4 P.M.

- Tenth column: "shooting or falling of the leaves of trees, of flours [flowers], and other remarkable plants"

- Eleventh column: record the "appearance or disappearance of birds, their emigrations, etc."

- Twelfth column: record anything else worth noting

"It will be an amusement to you and may become useful," wrote Jefferson. "I do not know whether you have a thermometer or barometer. If you have not, those columns will be unfilled till you can supply yourself." Jefferson was not letting his friend wriggle off the hook!

Lewis and Clark brought back drawings and samples of many types of plants from their expedition. Different trees have distinct leaves, fruit (pods, nuts), shapes, and bark that identify them.

WHAT YOU NEED

Assorted leaves

Waxed paper or foil

Newspaper

Stiff sheet of cardboard or plywood

Heavy books

Tree identification book or online sources

Clear-drying glue

Pen

Three-ring binder with paper

Collect a variety of leaves. Leaves can be simple, with one blade, or compound, with multiple blades on one stem. There are nearly 30 different types of leaf shapes. Collect a complete, undamaged leaf from each new tree you find. Most trees can be identified by their leaves. Different types of trees in the same family have different leaves. A pin oak leaf is different from a white oak leaf.

To dry each leaf, find a flat surface like a floor space or tabletop. Lay out waxed paper or foil. Then place a layer of several unfolded newspaper sheets. Lay your leaves on top. Don't let them touch. Put on another layer of newspaper topped with leaves, and so on until all your leaves are laid out. Top the last layer of newspaper with a thick sheet of heavy cardboard (or plywood) cut to the same size as the newspapers. Stack heavy books

or bricks on top. Let the leaves dry for at least one to two weeks.

The dried leaves will be fragile and brittle—don't over-handle them. Put a few drops of glue that dries clear on the leaf and stick it onto a sheet of paper. Press the leaf down until the glue dries by placing a sheet of waxed paper and a book on top of it.

Using a computer or a tree identification book, search and identify each type of leaf. Write a label next to each leaf. Include the tree's common name and the scientific Latin name. You can also include what type of fruit the tree makes and what region of the country the tree grows in.

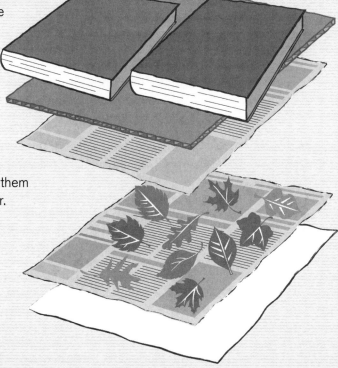

You can mount your leaves as art or group them into a three-ring binder.

of particular birds, reptiles, or insects." The Corps of Discovery should also record their meetings with Native Americans, noting tribal names, languages, traditions, and how they lived.

The Lewis and Clark expedition departed in May 1804. Congress provided funds for scientific instruments, small trade goods for Native Americans, camping gear, and medicines.

The tremendous trek of 8,000 miles to the Pacific Ocean and back kept Jefferson anxiously waiting two years for results. In spring 1805 the team wrote Jefferson about the expedition's first year. But after they left Fort Mandan in April, in what is now North Dakota, Jefferson heard no word from Lewis or Clark. He often worried about the fate of the men he'd sent to explore the vast American West. Their safe arrival home in St. Louis in September 1806 filled him with "unspeakable joy."

Jefferson could not wait to hear their stories! The expedition carried home journals filled with drawings and records of an amazing 122 species and subspecies of animals and 178 plants never previously described.

BRITISH TROUBLES, BURR PROBLEMS

Jefferson faced the presidential election of 1804 in deep mourning. His beautiful Polly had died following complications from childbirth on April 17. She left behind her husband, her little boy Francis Wayles Eppes, and her infant daughter, named Maria. This fresh loss staggered Jefferson. His only hopes for happiness, he wrote John Page, "now hang on the slender thread of a single life." As that slender thread, Martha stood steadfastly beside her father and, with her 11 children, surrounded him with loving family for the rest of his life. But Jefferson never completely recovered from Polly's death. Her baby daughter died a few years later.

Voters returned Thomas Jefferson to the presidency in a landslide victory. The electoral votes were 162 for Jefferson and 14 for Charles Cotesworth Pinckney. George Clinton replaced Aaron Burr as vice president. Back in July, Vice President Burr had challenged Alexander Hamilton to a duel and shot and killed the former Federalist leader.

In early 1806 Jefferson heard rumors about Aaron Burr and a fantastical plot. Burr planned to

Lewis and Clark carried a series of peace medals, from two to four inches across, to present to Native American leaders they'd meet on their journey. The medals were the first to show an American president. One side of the medal had Jefferson's profile, the other side showed the clasped hands of a Native American and white man with a crossed peace pipe and tomahawk. The medals were made of two rounds of hollow silver joined together.

ADULT SUPERVISION REQUIRED

WHAT YOU NEED

Rolling pin

Bakeable sculpting clay (like Sculpey)

2 drinking glasses in different sizes

Kitchen knife

Nail or toothpick

Spray paint

Glitter and glue (optional)

Roll out a piece of clay to the desired size and use the larger drinking glass to press down on the clay and make a circle. Trim with the kitchen knife.

Press the smaller drinking glass into the clay, making an edge around the medal.

Think about symbols of peace: a dove, an olive branch, a rainbow, whatever means peace to you. Use leftover pieces of clay to make symbols or figures to press onto the medal. Use the nail or toothpick to draw or press a design into the medal.

Bake the clay according to package directions, usually in a 275°F oven for 15 minutes for every ¼-inch thickness.

Spray paint your medal silver, bronze, or gold. Add touches of glitter with glue if desired.

Aaron Burr shoots Alexander Hamilton in a duel, July 11, 1804. Hamilton died the next day.
LIBRARY OF CONGRESS

set up an independent nation under his rule in the Spanish-held lands of the Southwest. Faced with continuing troubles from Great Britain and the wars sweeping Europe, Jefferson dismissed the Burr stories. Britain smashed the French navy at the Battle of Trafalgar, though Napoleon's armies controlled much of Europe. "What an awful spectacle does the world exhibit," lamented Jefferson in January 1806, "one man bestriding the continent of Europe like a Colossus and another roaming unbridled on the ocean."

Bold and unrestrained, British warships stopped and searched American ships hunting for British sailors who'd deserted from the harsh treatment of the British Navy. But the British also seized, or "impressed," American sailors. Events at sea only worsened. Britain continually harassed US shipping and blocked American vessels carrying French goods from anchoring in French colonies.

In June 1807, off the coast of Virginia, the British ship *Leopard* demanded to board the American vessel *Chesapeake*. They knew a few British deserters lurked on the *Chesapeake*. When the American captain refused, the *Leopard* opened fire, killing three sailors and wounding more. The *Chesapeake* surrendered and the British seized their deserters along with a few American sailors. Outrage swept across the country and Jefferson ordered all British ships out of American waters.

In autumn 1806 further information landed on Jefferson's desk about Burr's activities to recruit an army to lead against Spanish possessions in the Southwest. Jefferson issued a proclamation warning of the plot and ordering any expedition stopped. By March 1807 Burr was arrested, taken to Virginia, and charged with treason. Chief Justice John Marshall presided over the trial, and he ruled in Burr's favor on several important legal issues. The jury found Burr "not proved to be guilty under this indictment by any evidence submitted to us" and released him. Infuriated by the outcome, Jefferson condemned both the jury and the chief justice.

The president fumed at Marshall's "zeal for the liberty of those whom we would not permit to overthrow the liberties of the country." The government attempted to try Burr again. Once more, Burr earned an acquittal. Again seething, Jefferson felt that Marshall ignored the law and acted upon political beliefs. But in his wrath against Burr, Jefferson disregarded the real lack of evidence.

THE HATED EMBARGO

By the end of 1807 Napoleon blockaded American ships from French ports and authorized French ships to seize American vessels. The world's two warring superpowers strangled American trade in their mighty grip. This "great and increasing danger" to American sailors, ships, and goods spurred Jefferson to sign an Embargo Act closing all American ports to foreign trade. Americans could only trade with one another up and down the coast.

Jefferson hoped France and Britain might feel the pinch of going without American goods. But Britain and France did not suffer—America did, as the nation's trade collapsed and the economy fell in shambles. Looking for ways to avoid the embargo, Americans resorted to smuggling goods through Canada or the Caribbean and trading with the British and Spanish in the West. Angered—even disillusioned—Jefferson dug in more deeply. "While honest men were religiously observing it [the embargo], the unprincipled along our sea-coast and our frontier [have been] fraudulently evading it." In March 1808 he closed not only Atlantic shipping, but all overland and river routes, too.

Cartoon shows Jefferson saying, "This is a grand philosophical idea," while Americans complain their families are starving and their goods spoiling due to the Embargo Act.
COURTESY OF LIBRARY OF CONGRESS

Jefferson's actions particularly riled merchants in the old Federalist stronghold of New England, but the embargo also angered southerners who shipped their crops to Europe. Jefferson's opponents gleefully pointed out that Jefferson had once accused George III of the same abuses he now committed. Letters of protest poured into the White House, even from men who closed with: "Signed A True Republican." The embargo proved nearly impossible to enforce. Jefferson had not expected such a bitter response. As one of his last acts as president, Jefferson repealed the embargo.

PLAY A WORD GAME

One of Jefferson's great-granddaughters described how the family played word games in the evenings. "I Love My Love with an A" was one of their favorites.

WHAT YOU NEED

2 or more people

Gather friends and family and sit in a circle. This is an alphabet game that goes around the circle from person to person. The game progresses at a quick tempo through the alphabet. If someone makes a mistake or takes too long to think, they are out. They game continues until one person is left.

To play, repeat this phrase with each letter, beginning with A. The phrase "sign of the . . ." referred to the sign on a restaurant or tavern. "I love my love with an A. I took him (or her) to the sign of the *Antelope*, and I treated him to *Almonds*." The next person might say: "I love my love with a B. I took him to the sign of the *Bear*, and I treated him to *Biscuits*." Continue with the rest of the alphabet!

"TRANQUIL PURSUITS"

On March 4, 1809, 65-year-old Jefferson retired from public office. He watched his dear friend James Madison become the next president. But for himself, "never did a prisoner released from his chains feel such relief as I shall on shaking off the shackles of power." Now, Monticello called him home to be with his daughter and his grandchildren, his sister, his nieces, and his nephews. It had been 40 years since he'd arrived in Williamsburg for his first session in the House of Burgesses. Jefferson planned to bury himself in the heart of his family and "the tranquil pursuits of science," his "supreme delight."

Martha and her family lived nearby. Eventually she moved in to run the household for her father. Jefferson doted on his grandchildren. He led explorations through the gardens and supervised races on the lawn, dropping his handkerchief to start the runners off. The victors won treats of dried fruit. In the evenings, before darkness fell and the candles were lit, the family played games. As his granddaughters became young women, Jefferson bought them their first silk dresses and watched proudly as they married at Monticello. As the years passed, Jefferson relied more, too, on his grandson Thomas Jefferson Randolph, called Jeff, to manage his farms.

Jefferson rode his horse, Old Eagle, daily. The former president cut his gray hair short to save the bother of tying it back, and outdoors donned a wide-brimmed hat to shield his face. He often wore red, the bright color enhancing visitors' opinions that he seemed younger than his years.

The innovative "stew stove" in Monticello's kitchen.
MONTICELLO/THOMAS JEFFERSON FOUNDATION, INC.

As Jefferson grew older his sight and hearing remained good. He dined on little meat, preferring vegetables. He experimented with and grew 330 varieties of more than 70 types of vegetables in his 1,000-foot-long kitchen garden, terraced into a hillside by Monticello slaves. He gathered the seeds and stored them, carefully labeled, in small hanging glass bottles or tins. Jefferson also planned and tended his

flower gardens. He loved everything about gardening and wrote to artist Charles Willson Peale, "But tho an old man, I am but a young gardener."

Monticello boasted one of the most modern kitchens in the country. Edy Fossett and Fanny Gillette roasted meats and stirred large pots in the huge open fireplace. Breads baked in the built-in oven. Most innovative, a "stew stove" with six charcoal burners allowed delicate sauces to simmer over hot coals. Jefferson introduced many of his guests to ice cream, pasta, capers, olives, and fine white wines.

But the years of entertaining scores of visitors and curiosity seekers further drained Jefferson's finances. Overseer Edmund Bacon described "a perfect throng" of guests constantly descending on Monticello. The hoards "used up all his income from the plantation and everything else," complained Bacon, "but he was so kind and polite that he received all his visitors with a smile and made them welcome." Jefferson's granddaughter Ellen recalled some evenings when 50 guests showed up expecting food, entertainment, and a bed for the night! As a Virginia gentlemen Jefferson could not slam the door in anyone's face.

Jefferson kept busy with many projects. Young law students boarding in nearby Charlottesville arrived to pick Jefferson's brain and visit his law library. Jefferson began collecting papers from his time as secretary of state and starting penning his thoughts into an autobiography.

He continued work on *The Life and Morals of Jesus of Nazareth*, a personal collection of what he

Poplar Forest. The parlor's long windows look out on the sunken lawn. To the side, the dependencies where servants worked, such as the kitchen and laundry, were hidden under the walkway terrace.

COURTESY OF THOMAS JEFFERSON'S POPLAR FOREST/PHOTOGRAPH BY BRANDON MARIE MILLER

believed were the moral teachings of Jesus. He studied the gospels of Matthew, Mark, Luke, and John in different languages seeking "the most sublime and benevolent code of morals which has ever been offered to man." He separated the words of Jesus from those of "the unlettered apostles . . . and the Christians of the first century." He cut and pasted his favorite Gospel passages onto blank pages, creating a little book for himself and his family.

POPLAR FOREST

Jefferson resided in many houses in Philadelphia, in New York, in France, and at the President's House in Washington, D.C. But besides Monticello the only home he designed and built for himself was his intimate, little, octagon-shaped home at Poplar Forest. Building at Poplar Forest, 90 miles and a three-day journey away from Monticello, began in 1806. From 1809 on, Jefferson escaped here three or four times a year, with a grandchild or two in tow, from the endless visitors, scrutiny, and chaos that swirled around Monticello. Jefferson reveled in the "solitude of a hermit" at Poplar Forest, far from his "absent friends."

The dining room, a perfect 20-foot cube lit with a skylight, sat in the center of the house. Around the sides were Jefferson's bedroom, guest rooms, and a large sunlit parlor with floor-to-ceiling windows that opened onto a porch. Of course, Jefferson transported many beloved books to Poplar Forest; his collection here numbered nearly 1,000 titles! At one point his granddaughter Cornelia complained that she and her sister Ellen must "put numbers on all of grandpapa's books & it will take us nearly the whole day which I am very sorry for."

As at Monticello a terrace wing stretched out from one side of the house with the dependencies, where servants worked—kitchen, laundry, smokehouse, cook's room, and storage—underneath. "About twilight of the evening," wrote Jefferson, "we sally out with the owls and bats and take our evening exercise on the terras [terrace]."

At this working plantation, Jefferson grew tobacco, wheat, and corn. In the house only a few servants tended Jefferson and his family, though he always brought his trusted butler, Burwell Colbert—another member of the Hemings clan—from Monticello. Jefferson enjoyed time to read at leisure at Poplar Forest. He pursued interesting problems like making a "geometrical measurement" of a nearby mountain range or calculating the latitude of his plantation. He walked, engaged his grandchildren in long conversations, planned Poplar Forest's gardens, and relaxed. As granddaughter Ellen later recalled, "At Poplar Forest he found in a pleasant home, rest, leisure, power to carry on his favorite pursuits—to think, to study, to read."

LETTERS

In every year of his retirement Jefferson received at least 1,000 letters, and he answered most of them. He often used a machine called a polygraph that had two connected pens; the writer would use one pen and the second would mimic those movements to make an exact copy on a second sheet of paper (see the photo on p. 120). In January 1812 the handwriting on one envelope must have caught Jefferson's heart. John Adams, his dear old friend, his one-time enemy, a man he had not corresponded with for many years, had written to him! Politics had crushed their friendship, but now in retirement, Adams and Jefferson rekindled their ties. It would be a shame, as Adams wrote later, if they should die without having explained themselves to each other. Jefferson wrote back a long letter, remarking on their many years as "fellow laborers in the same cause." He confided his joy that "I live in the midst of my grandchildren."

Over the course of 158 letters, they penned their versions of the American Revolution. They touched on their children and grandchildren. They discussed political theory, religion, philosophy, the aging process, and what books they read. Time had not softened their views, however—they still disagreed on many points. But now, it mattered

DAB A THEOREM PAINTING

Theorem painting was popular with genteel young ladies in the early 1800s. Jefferson's daughters and granddaughters probably dabbled in the art. It uses a series of stencils to paint a picture on fabric. Theorem painting is usually done on white cotton velvet using oil paints, but practice first on white felt with acrylic colors.

ADULT SUPERVISION REQUIRED

WHAT YOU NEED

Pencil

Plain sheet of white paper

Ruler

Sheets of tracing paper

Piece of heavy cardboard

Craft knife

Piece of white cotton velvet or felt

Spray adhesive

Paints (acrylics or oils)

Fine-tipped paintbrush, stencil paintbrush
  (a round, flat brush), or soft flannel pieces

Plate covered with aluminum foil

Paper towels

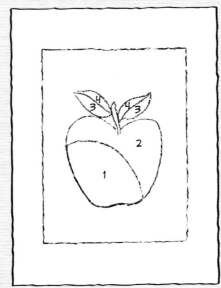

Sketch out your painting design on a plain sheet of paper. Popular subjects for theorem paintings include fruits, flowers, birds, and animals. Decide what colors will fill in each section of the drawing. Number each section that will be the same color with the same number. All the reds are #1, the dark blues #2, and so on. With a ruler, draw a rectangle around your drawing like a frame.

Lay a sheet of tracing paper on top of your drawing. Trace the frame and all the #1s. Then set that sheet aside and use a new sheet. Trace the frame and all the #2s. Keep going, using a new sheet for each number.

Lay each sheet of tracing paper on a piece of heavy cardboard. Use a craft knife to carefully cut out each numbered shape. Turn the cardboard as you outline the shape with

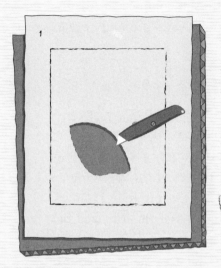

the craft knife to make it easier. Then peel the center out. The open space is the stencil you will use to paint. Put the number in the corner of the paper so you know which piece of the pattern it is. Continue cutting out all the shapes on the separate sheets of tracing paper.

Cut the fabric to fit your stencil frame. Spray adhesive onto the cardboard and smooth your fabric on top. Let dry.

Squeeze a small dab of your first paint color onto the foil-covered plate. Paint the stencils in order from

background to foreground. Lay the first stencil on the fabric. Dab your brush into the paint and roll it around on the foil. The brush should be dry, not dripping with paint, which can seep under the paper stencil. Rub the brush lightly on a paper towel if it is too wet. Hold the brush straight up and down and rub the paint onto the fabric, starting at the edges and working in. It should have a soft, delicate effect. (Instead of a brush you can also use pieces of soft flannel wrapped around your pointer finger to dab on the paint.)

After you have painted all the #1s onto the fabric, remove the stencil. Let dry if needed. Line up the second stencil with the patterns fitting as on your original drawing. Paint as before, using all your stencils to fill in the picture.

When you have stenciled in all the colors, use the fine-tipped brush dipped in black paint to fill in between sections, adding details and outlines.

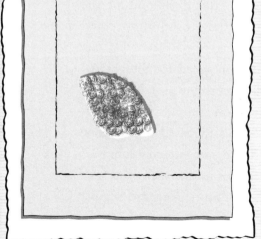

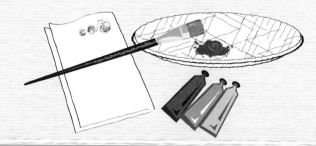

Jefferson's cabinet, or study, at Monticello held many of his scientific instruments, his polygraph or copying machine, and his revolving bookstand. In this room Jefferson read, made architectural drawings and scientific observations, and wrote thousands of pages.

MONTICELLO/PHOTOGRAPH BY ROBERT LAUTMAN

less. "We are both too old to change opinions," Jefferson acknowledged, "which are the result of a long life."

When the British burned Washington, D.C., during the War of 1812, Jefferson offered to replace the destroyed Library of Congress with his own collection of 6,500 books. Congress purchased Jefferson's library in 1815 for $23,950. Always deeply in debt, Jefferson needed the money. But as the wagons packed with volumes rumbled away from Monticello, an empty Jefferson confided to Adams, "I cannot live without books," and promptly began buying more.

"THE WOLF BY THE EARS"

Jefferson bothered little with politics, though his friend James Monroe followed Madison as president. Jefferson did, however, worry about the union and about the gathering power of the central government. In spring of 1820 he wrote John Holmes, a congressman from Maine. Jefferson criticized the Missouri Compromise, a bill that maintained the union's balance of slave and free states. Missouri entered the union as a new slave state, while Maine entered as a new free state.

But Jefferson viewed the scalding debates over slavery in Congress as a means for northern and western states to threaten the livelihood of the South. Jefferson believed the Constitution could not be used to limit the spread of slavery.

The days when Jefferson called for the gradual abolition of slavery belonged to the past. Now slavery loomed as a problem too complex and dangerous to be solved. "We have the wolf by the ears, and we can neither hold him, nor safely let him go," he wrote Holmes. "Justice is in one scale, and self-preservation in the other." Future generations must find the solution to slavery.

"But this momentous question, like a fire bell in the night, awakened and filled me with terror.

I considered it at once as the knell of the Union," he wrote Holmes. The Missouri Compromise hushed the issue, "but it is a reprieve only, not a final sentence. . . . I regret that I am now to die," Jefferson wrote sadly, "in the belief that the useless sacrifice of themselves by the generation of 1776 to acquire self-government and happiness to their country is to be thrown away by the unwise and unworthy passions of their sons, and that my only consolation is to be that I live not to weep over it."

When a young abolitionist wrote Jefferson a few years later asking the former president to support the cause, Jefferson declined. "This enterprise is for the young, for those who can follow it up and bear it through to its consummation. It shall have all my prayers, and these are the only weapons of an old man."

UNIVERSITY OF VIRGINIA

Though Jefferson called himself a "monument of another age," he still looked to the future. His long-cherished views remained that mankind progressed slowly but surely, lifted by education and scientific discoveries onto a new plateau where evils like slavery would one day no longer exist. He held tight to his belief in public education and plunged into a new and energizing project—planning a university that he hoped would become "the most eminent in the United States."

Every aspect of the university, both large and small, captivated Jefferson. He designed a domed library using Palladio's descriptions of the ancient Pantheon in Rome. The great rotunda would stand

The Rotunda, designed by Jefferson, at the University of Virginia.

guard over a sweep of green lawn and an academic village where students would learn and live alongside their professors.

Jefferson outlined schedules and penned reading lists. He hired teachers from Europe, insisting no clergymen serve on his faculty. He drafted rules for students and teachers and required students learn "the principles of government."

Jefferson's dear friend Lafayette visited in 1824 and attended the November opening ceremonies for the University of Virginia. Eighty-one-year-old Jefferson dined with guests beneath the great dome he'd designed. The next spring the first students moved into the "Academical Village." But their rowdy and riotous behavior crushed Jefferson. At a

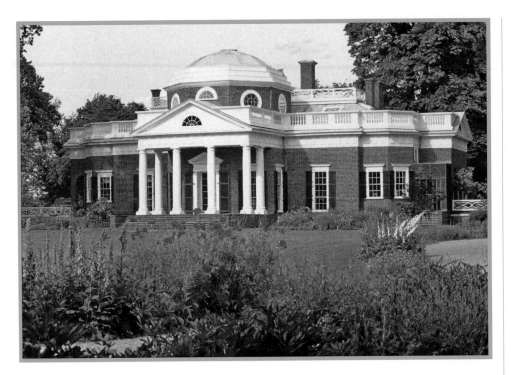

The West Front of Monticello in summer.
MONTICELLO/PHOTOGRAPH BY MARY PORTER

meeting with the students a disheartened Jefferson, sick with disappointment, wept. His tears more than anything shamed the young men to behave better.

"A DEADLY BLAST TO MY PEACE OF MIND"

How to save his family from his sinking hole of debt tormented Jefferson in the dark hours of night. Jefferson had cosigned a loan for a friend in March 1819, meaning Jefferson would pay if the friend could not. By August, his friend defaulted on the loan, sticking Jefferson with the original loan plus $1,200 a year in interest payments—a new threat piled on top of his own staggering debt accumulated over a lifetime.

Then in 1825 the economy crashed. Land values, crop prices, and the value of paper money all toppled. Jefferson's life toppled, too. He devised a plan to sell some of his lands and his nail-making business in a lottery. This way he hoped to pocket at least a fair price for his land.

Jefferson approached friends in the Virginia Assembly for the right to sell lottery tickets. At first the legislature refused, and with a heavy heart Jefferson wrote his grandson Jeff in February 1826: "I see, in the failure of this hope, a deadly blast to my peace of mind during my remaining days. I should not care were life to end with the line I am writing, were it not that I may yet be of some avail to the family." In the end, the legislature agreed to the lottery but Jefferson would have to sell Monticello, the furnishings, the slaves, the horses—everything. He could live at Monticello the rest of his days, but Martha and her children would never inherit Monticello, the passion and joy of his life. This great blow saddened the elderly Jefferson. And there was no question about him freeing his slaves—he could not afford it.

Jefferson enjoyed good health well into old age. But during the early months of 1826 he kept mostly to his couch, suffering with diabetes, infections, and arthritis in his joints. He wrote "slowly and with difficulty." He described himself as "weakened in body by infirmities and in mind by age, now far gone into my 83rd year, reading one newspaper only and forgetting immediately what I read." He

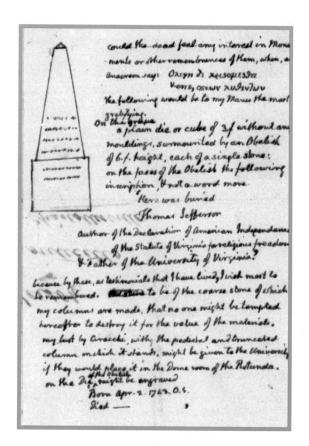

Jefferson's plan for his grave marker and epitaph.
COURTESY OF LIBRARY OF CONGRESS

wrote his will, leaving each grandchild a watch, a gold-headed walking stick to James Madison, Poplar Forest to his grandson Francis Eppes, his books to the University of Virginia, and all his personal papers to Jeff, including over 25,000 letters and account books.

"THEN FAREWELL"

On July 1, Jefferson began drifting in and out of consciousness. His doctor dosed him with a mixture

Burwell's Purchases

Burwell's Purchases

Thomas Jefferson died more than $105,000 in debt—nearly $2 million in today's money. Within six months of his death the auction sales began for the house, all the furnishings, and 130 enslaved people. Burwell Colbert, Jefferson's trusted slave, bought a carving knife, a canister of tea, a print of Lafayette, a pair of pitchers, and a mule from his former master's estate. Colbert's loyalty and work had been so exemplary that Jefferson paid him a salary of $20 a year. In his will, Jefferson wrote, "I give to my good, affectionate, and faithful servant Burwell his freedom, and the sum of three hundred Dollars."

of opium and honey for the pain. Jefferson tossed and turned. "This is the fourth of July?" he asked more than once. He willed his body to go on, the hours slipping away, edging nearer to the momentous date. Burwell Colbert, his family, and his doctor hovered close by.

On July 4, 1826, the 50th anniversary of the Declaration of Independence, Thomas Jefferson died as the clock approached one o'clock in the afternoon. Hundreds of miles away, in one of the greatest coincidences in American history, John Adams, Jefferson's fellow warrior of 1776, died too.

That day at Monticello, America lost a complicated man. A man who believed in frugal government yet lived his own life burdened by debt. A man who hated kings and privileged nobles yet lived as an aristocrat himself. A man who believed passionately in freedom and liberty yet owned slaves who toiled for his comfort.

the charge against slavery, fighting for women's rights, fighting for civil rights.

His family buried Jefferson next to his wife, Martha. Atop his grave stood a gray stone monument, designed by Jefferson and listing the accomplishments "by which I most wish to be remembered." There appears no mention of his two terms as president or his service as vice president, secretary of state, or minister to France. Instead the obelisk proclaims:

> Here was buried
> Thomas Jefferson
> author of the
> Declaration
> of American Independence
> of the
> Statute of Virginia
> for
> Religious Freedom,
> and father of the
> University of Virginia.

Jefferson was a complex, brilliant man—an architect, a scientist, a writer, a dreamer, the supreme believer in freedom from government. He penned the words most resonant throughout our history, the best statement of the American creed, that all people are "created equal, with certain unalienable Rights." Most shining of these rights is the right to liberty. The echoes from Jefferson's mighty pen floated like banners for future Americans leading

A week before his death Jefferson wrote his last public letter, marking the 50th anniversary of the Declaration of Independence. "May it be to the world what I believe it will be," he wrote, "to some parts sooner, to others later, but finally to all, the signal to assume the blessings and security of self-government. . . . All eyes are opened, or opening, to the rights of man. . . . For ourselves, let the annual return of this day forever refresh our recollection of these rights, and an undiminished devotion to them."

PLACES TO VISIT AND WEBSITES TO EXPLORE

THOMAS JEFFERSON'S MONTICELLO

Learn about Thomas Jefferson, his family, and the African Americans who called Monticello home. Year-round programs and exhibits, kids' activities, and tours highlight Jefferson as an architect, statesman, family man, gardener, and naturalist.

931 Thomas Jefferson Parkway
Charlottesville, Virginia 22902
(434) 984-9822

For a virtual tour and a wealth of information on Jefferson and life at Monticello visit www.monticello.org.

THOMAS JEFFERSON'S POPLAR FOREST

Visit the only other home Jefferson designed and built for himself, his personal retreat. Tours and activities for kids including summer camps and archaeology field school. Open April–November.

1542 Bateman Bridge Road
Forest, Virginia 24551-0419
(434) 525-1806

For a virtual tour and more information on Jefferson's life at Poplar Forest visit www.poplarforest.org.

INDEPENDENCE NATIONAL HISTORIC PARK

Visit the meeting place for the Continental Congress, the spot where the Declaration of Independence was debated and adopted. Special programs; includes other historic sites like the Liberty Bell and the Franklin Court printing office.

Visitor Center
525 Market Street
Philadelphia, Pennsylvania 19106
(215) 965-2305

For more information visit www.nps.gov/inde/index.htm.

COLONIAL WILLIAMSBURG

Stroll the same streets as Thomas Jefferson, visit the Capitol, where the House of Burgesses met, tour the Governor's Palace and George Wythe's house, and peek in the Apollo Room of the Raleigh Tavern. Museums, living history, special programs.

PO Box 1776
Williamsburg, Virginia 23187-1776
(800) HISTORY

Find out more about the people and places of colonial Williamsburg at www.history.org.

LIBRARY OF CONGRESS

Visit http://memory.loc.gov/ammem/collections/jefferson_papers/ to view the Thomas Jefferson Papers. An online exhibit catalog with Jefferson objects is available at www.loc.gov/exhibits/jefferson/object.html.

FURTHER READING FOR YOUNG PEOPLE

* Bernstein, R. B. *Thomas Jefferson: The Revolution of Ideas*. New York: Oxford University Press, 2004.

* Bober, Natalie. *Thomas Jefferson: Draftsman of a Nation*. Charlottesville: University of Virginia Press, 2007.

Ching, Jacqueline. *Thomas Jefferson*. New York: DK Publishing, 2009.

Herbert, Janis. *The American Revolution for Kids*. Chicago: Chicago Review Press, 2002.

Miller, Brandon Marie. *Benjamin Franklin, American Genius*. Chicago: Chicago Review Press, 2009.

———. *Declaring Independence: Life During the American Revolution*. Minneapolis: Lerner Publishing, 2005.

———. *George Washington for Kids*. Chicago: Chicago Review Press, 2007.

Severance, John. *Thomas Jefferson: Architect of Democracy*. New York: Clarion, 1998.

* YOUNG ADULT TITLE

Selected Bibliography

Bedini, Silvio. *Jefferson and Science*. Chapel Hill, NC: Thomas Jefferson Foundation, 2002. Distributed by University of North Carolina Press.

Beiswanger, William, with Peter Hatch, Lucia Stanton, and Susan Stein. *Thomas Jefferson's Monticello*. Chapel Hill, NC: Thomas Jefferson Foundation, 2002. Distributed by University of North Carolina Press.

Bernstein, R. B. *Thomas Jefferson*. New York: Oxford University Press, 2003.

Breig, James. "Hair's Breadth: Locks Could Be the Key to Jefferson Mystery." *Colonial Williamsburg Journal*, Autumn 2010.

Ellis, Joseph P. *American Sphinx: The Character of Thomas Jefferson*. New York: Vintage Books, 1998.

Horn, Joan. *Thomas Jefferson's Poplar Forest: A Private Place*. Forest, VA: Corporation for Jefferson's Poplar Forest, 2002.

Jefferson, Thomas. *Writings*. Edited by Merrill D. Peterson. New York: Library of America, 1984.

Stanton, Lucia. *Free Some Day: The African-American Families of Monticello*. Charlottesville, VA: Thomas Jefferson Foundation, 2000.

Thomas Jefferson Encyclopedia. Thomas Jefferson Foundation, n.d., www.monticello.org/site/research-and-collections/tje.

Van Pelt, Charles. "Thomas Jefferson and Maria Cosway." *American Heritage* 22, no. 5 (August 1971).

Wilson, Gaye. "Monticello Was Among the Prizes in a Lottery for a Ruined Jefferson's Relief." *Colonial Williamsburg Journal*, Winter 2010.

INDEX